"Prayer is where the action is."

John Wesley

This Book is Dedicated to:

My parents, Mr. and Mrs. Charlie Lewis Sr., who poured into me love, support, and a firm foundation in God.

Helen C. Smith, whose critical eye for editing helped me find my writing "voice."

Drs. Jeremy A. Ross and Julie Reznicek, the medical angels who restored my health, enabling me to write this book.

My sister, the late Wanda F. Lewis Hendrix. I love you and continue to hold you with me every day.

My aunt, the late Reverend Essie C. Simmons, who modeled for me the first lessons in being a pastor.

My siblings, Le'Ontyne, Charlene, Reta, and Charlie, for always having my back.

Kevin Slimp (publisher at Market Square Books), Kristin Lighter (editor), and Ken Rochelle (post-production editor), for giving me the opportunity to bless others through my writing.

Journey to Transformation

2020 Lenten Devotional

Bishop Sharma D. Lewis

Market
Square
BOOKS

Journey to Transformation
2020 Lenten Devotional

©2019 Bishop Sharma Lewis

books@marketsquarebooks.com
P.O. Box 23664 Knoxville, Tennessee 37933

ISBN: 978-1-950899-08-1
Library of Congress: 2019951478

Printed and Bound in the United States of America
Cover Illustration & Book Design ©2019 Market Square Publishing, LLC

Publisher: Kevin Slimp
Editor: Kristin Lighter
Post-Process Editor: Ken Rochelle
Special Thanks to: Faye Goolrick

Unless noted otherwise, Scripture quotations are from:

Table of Contents

Introduction
Looking Ahead to Lent

Lent is a season of forty days, not counting Sundays, that begins on Ash Wednesday and ends on Holy Saturday. This season is a forty-day period of repentance and renewal preceding Easter. It allows us as believers of Christ to recall the Easter Story and understand its meaning: that our Lord and Savior lived and died to redeem the world from sin. Because of Christ's death and resurrection, our lives can be renewed as we have the power to renounce sin and begin to live for God. Historically, Lent began as a period of fasting and preparation for Holy Baptism by converts, then became a time for penance by all Christians.[1]

Today, Ash Wednesday emphasizes two themes: we confront our own mortality, and we confess our sin before God within the community of faith. The use of ashes as a sign of mortality and repentance has a long history in Jewish and Christian tradition. I invite you to participate in an Ash Wednesday Experience. The Imposition of Ashes is a powerful and experiential way of participating

---

1 *UMC Book of Worship.* The United Methodist Publishing House. 1992.

in the call to repentance and reconciliation.[2]

As we journey together for the next six weeks, I invite you to observe Lent by introspection, repentance, forgiveness, renewal, prayer, fasting, and Biblical Study. This study is divided into four sections: Lenten Devotional, Prayer, Reflection, and My Action. Since Lent is a time for self-examination and renewal, I offer a My Action section each day to allow you to continue to put into practice what you have read and reflected upon, and as an opportunity to transform someone's life.

Since Sundays are not counted during the Lenten season, this study will allow you or a group to further engage in introspection. On Sundays, My Personal Reflections Notes will ask you to reflect and journal on the past week's study with the following questions: (a) Which day stood out during this Lenten journey? (b) What did you learn about yourself and your relationship with Jesus Christ? and (c) under the heading of My Action – Which day brought you great joy or difficulty? Why? Please journal your thoughts.

2   Ibid.

February 26, 2020

Ash Wednesday

Matthew 6:1-6, 16-21

Today's text, found in Matthew 6:1-6, 16-21, challenges us to provide ministry to the poor and to develop a life of prayer and fasting. However, we are cautioned that if we participate in these spiritual acts, we must have the right motivation. Jesus spoke to this issue when he said, "Be careful not to do your acts of righteousness before men to be seen by them. If you do, you will have no reward from your Father in heaven" (Matthew 6:1). Proverbs 16:2 states ". . . all a person's ways seem pure to them, but motives are weighed by the Lord." The Lord is not interested in our selfish acts or motives, but discerns our thoughts and intentions of the heart.[3]

Furthermore, as we witness in the text, selfish motives can hinder our prayers. Jesus said, ". . . do not be like the hypocrites for they love to pray standing in the synagogues and on the street corners to be seen by men." Interestingly, the Greek word *hypocrite* means "one acting a part," as if a character in a play. Sixteen of the twenty-seven uses of this word in the New Testament are found in Matthew, which characterizes the hypocrite as a

---

3   Hebrews 4:12.

person whose actions are intended to impress observers[4] and whose spiritual-sounding talk hides corrupt motives.[5] In Matthew 6, we are told prayer is to be meditative and not boastful. Prayer is a manifestation of an intimate relationship with Jesus Christ. Our prayer life should be a daily, consistent discipline that fosters a deep communion with God. Our focus in Matthew 6:6 encourages us to "go into your room, close the door and pray to the Father, who is unseen."

Prayer has deepened my faith and has been my anchor and lifeline to God. Through spending countless hours in my "prayer closet," I have experienced the loving grace of God's presence. My life and ministry have been enriched by seeking God's face in the posture of praying. One of my favorite quotes by Richard Foster, author of *Prayer: Finding the Heart's True Home*, is "The primary purpose of prayer is to bring us into such a life of communion with the Father that, by the power of the Spirit, we are increasingly conformed to the image of the Son." [6]

Jesus speaks in the text about the motivation of fasting. "When you fast, do not look somber as the hypocrites do, for they disfigure their faces to show men they are fasting." As a religious obligation, many religious leaders fasted twice a week for twelve hours. Jesus did not disapprove of the practice of fasting. What He disapproved of was those who publicized their fasts for personal attention

---

4   Matthew 6:1-3,16-18.

5   Richards, Lawrence O. *Devotional Commentary*, Cook Communications Ministries, Colorado Springs, 2002, p. 645.

6   Foster, Richard. *Prayer: Finding the Heart's True Home*. HarperCollins. 1992.

or wrong motives. Isaiah 58:5-7 gives clear insight on the understanding of fasting:

> *Is this kind of fast I have chosen, only a day for people to humble themselves? Is it only for bowing one's head like a reed and for lying in sackcloth and ashes? Is that what you call a fast, a day acceptable to the Lord? Is not this the kind of fasting I have chosen: to loosen the chains of injustice and untie the cords of the yoke, to set the oppressed free and break every yoke? Is it not to share your food with the hungry and to provide the poor wanderer with shelter – when you see the naked, to clothe them, and not to turn away from your own flesh and blood?*

We must be careful as we journey this Lenten season that our motives in drawing closer to God are pure and that the Lenten season is not a yearly habitual act.

One may ask what is the right motivation? Paul speaks in 1 Thessalonians 2:4, ". . . we are not trying to please people but God, who tests our hearts." The Lord is interested in our motives even more than our actions. The Apostle Paul says in 1 Corinthians 4:5 that we should ". . . wait until the Lord comes. He will bring to light what is hidden in darkness and will expose the motives of the heart. At that time each will receive their praise from God." We can keep our motives pure by continually surrendering our hearts and lives to Jesus Christ.

Prayer

Lord, for the next forty days please allow me to surrender all my impure motives in my life. May I seek you first and work towards a closer relationship with you, not only for this time of forty days, but going forward in life as well. Amen.

Reflection

What motivates you as a person, in life?

What happens when impure motives or thoughts crowd our thinking and action?

What impure motives have you had this past week?

My Action

Commit to working through this devotional individually or with a group. Spend time reflecting and reading the Bible for the next forty days.

February 27, 2020
Jonah 3:1-10

Are you obedient to warnings that are set before you? Do you immediately obey or disobey the instructions? Or do you see the instructions as a challenge?

Every Sunday my family would follow the "Lewis Sunday wake-up ritual" on command. First, my mother would awaken us by singing the gospel song, "May the Work I've Done Speak for Me."

There were times my brother and I thought about hiding this record, only to decide that probably wasn't a good idea. She would go throughout the house opening the blinds and calling our names to assure that we were up. If we wanted to get more sleep, it was interrupted by her singing and the smell of coffee, biscuits, and bacon from the kitchen. She would remind us that our clothes were ironed and placed at the foot of our beds.

During our breakfast time, Mom would check to see if our Sunday School lessons were completed. Finally, she would instruct us to go and sit in the front room so our clothes would not be dirty before church. This was not only our Sunday ritual, but the ritual to maintain clean clothes before an event. I never understood until I was older why my parents called our living room the front room. Simply, it was the first room (front room) in the house.

However, one Easter morning, when I was approximately eleven years old, my little brother decided not to obey the warning of getting his clothes dirty. Charlie was always testing my parents' rules because he was the youngest and mischievous. Did I mention he was the only boy of six children? We were dressed in our new Easter attire and Mom cautioned us to "sit still" in the front room. I have no idea to this day why my brother decided it was a good idea to go outside. He knew the Lewis ritual. He knew that Mom was adamant about us sitting in the front room. And he knew that Mom would kill him if he got dirty.

As soon as he walked outside, he slipped and fell and was covered with dirt from his head to his toes. At first I wanted to laugh, but I could see the look of fright on his face. There was nothing I could do but run outside and try to help him. Unfortunately, as I approached Charlie, I could feel my legs getting weak and before I could maintain my balance, I fell on top of him. There we lay on the ground laughing, dirty, and horrified that we were in trouble because we disobeyed a simple request. Needless to say, Mom heard the commotion before we could sneak back into the house. My dress was dirty, Charlie was scared, and Momma was angry. At first, I thought she was going to make us attend church in our dirty clothes. With a sharp tone she told us, "Change your clothes and I will deal with you all later." Sadly, this day was ruined because I kept wondering about our punishment and I couldn't wear my new Easter dress or shoes.

As we examine our text for today, Jonah was given instructions by God to tell the people of Nineveh to change from their wicked ways. With boldness and clarity, Jonah warned them that they had forty days to repent. If they did not, the city would be overthrown. According to the passage of scripture in verses 5-9, the people believed God, proclaimed a fast, and put on sackcloth. The people of Nineveh even repented on behalf of their animals. God witnessed their genuine repentance and decided not to destroy them. According to *Vine's Complete Expository Dictionary of Old and New Testament Words*, "repentance" means to have a change of the heart or disposition of one's conduct.

I don't think that my brother Charlie had repentance on his mind when he decided to go outside. He was being a typical seven-year-old who decided not to obey the warnings of his mother, but instead to receive her instructions as a challenge. Unfortunately, we were punished after church. Charlie never went outside again on a Sunday morning and I never followed him. This day was always etched in our minds to sit in the front room so our clothes would not be dirty: "because mother knows best."

Prayer

Lord, give me ears to hear, the will to listen, and the strength to obey your Word. Amen.

Reflection

Are you obedient to the warnings that are set before you?

My Action

Share a time that you were obedient and disobedient to a warning that was set before you. What were the outcomes?

February 28, 2020

Psalm 51

Psalm 51 is the most known of the penitential psalms. It is ordinarily classified as a prayer for help, or an individual lament or complaint. What sets it apart is that the psalmist's complaint involves his or her own sinfulness.

This scriptural text has become, over time, a meditation used to introduce the Season of Lent, a source for liturgy, and a text for reflection on the Christian doctrine of sin. Psalm 51 was written after the recorded incident in 2 Samuel chapters 11-12, when David committed adultery and murdered Uriah. David was definitely deserving of the death penalty for committing adultery and murder. However, David writes this psalm admitting his sinful nature and asking God for forgiveness. Forgiveness refers to God's pardoning the sins of human beings. Sin has permeated all of society and the Apostle Paul reminds us in Romans 3:23, ". . . that all have sinned and fall short of the glory of God."

The passage opens with an appeal to God and the acknowledgment of the sin committed. "Have mercy on me, O God, according to your unfailing love . . ." David doesn't justify his sin, he simply states it. What I find intriguing in today's passage is that before any mention of David's sin, the psalmist appeals to God's character using three key Hebrew words that communicate God's grace, mercy, and steadfast love. "Mercy is the aspect of God's love that causes God to help the miserable, just as grace is the aspect of God's love that moves God to forgive the guilty."[7] What I love about this passage is that this story displays the loving character of God's grace. God's grace is characterized as "favor or kindness shown without regard to the worth or merit of the one who receives it."[8] *Mercy* and *grace* are actions that show God's steadfast love for us.

After appealing to God's character, the psalmist turns to his own sinfulness. There are three words that denote the meaning of sin found in this passage: *iniquity* which involves the personal guilt, *transgression,* which suggests willful rebellion; and *evil,* which conveys the injurious effects of sinful behavior. David teaches us about forgiveness because he trusted God's grace and mercy.

In seeking God's forgiveness, we must first confess our sins. John the Evangelist states, "If we confess our sins, he is faithful and just to forgive us our sins and cleanse us from all unrighteousness" (1 John 1:9). When we confess our sins, we are acknowledging to God our human frailties and limitations. To confess is to admit that we are sinners in need of His grace and mercy. Sin is pervasive.

---

7   Youngblood, Ronald F., General Editor, *Nelson's New Illustrated Bible Dictionary,* Thomas Nelson Publishers, Nashville, 1995, p.#822.

8   ibid, p.#522.

We are born into it, and we cannot escape it.

Secondly, the confession of sin leads to repentance. This is one of the best examples of individual repentance in the Bible. David realized that not only did he sin against Bathsheba and Uriah; most importantly he sinned against God. Those who repent trust God's love to forgive. In the text, David asked God to cleanse him by doing three things: to remove his sin, to restore his joy, and to renew his spirit. David repeatedly calls for his cleansing, expressing his profound sense of guilt. The psalmist's faith in God's transforming power is particularly evident in verse 10, when he says, "Create in me a pure heart, O God."

Finally, repentance leads to restoration. It is God's fundamental character to restore, rehabilitate, and re-create sinners. In verse 12, David cries, "Restore to me the joy of your salvation, and grant me a willing spirit, to sustain me." God's Spirit is responsible for all life and its provisions. For the Psalmist David, to receive a new spirit and to live in the presence of the Holy Spirit means renewal.

Prayer

Lord, please forgive me of my sins. Create in me a clean heart. Amen.

Reflection

Why is it difficult for humanity to forgive themselves?

My Action

Read Psalm 51 aloud. Forgive yourself today and pray a prayer of repentance.

February 29, 2020

Matthew 18:1-7

Muhammad Ali was an American professional boxer, activist, and philanthropist. He was nicknamed "The Greatest" and widely respected as one of the most celebrated sports figures of the twentieth century, as well as one of the greatest boxers of all times. Before every match, it was customary for Ali to taunt his opponents by acknowledging openly that he was the fastest and the greatest of all champs. He would boast that given the chance, he was going to win the match by KO (Knock Out). Interestingly, out of sixty-one total fights, he won thirty-seven by knockout. I don't know that Muhammad Ali was thinking about the "greatest" in the sense of our word for today.

However, in the text, the disciples are questioning Jesus: "Who is the greatest in the kingdom of heaven?" Jesus instructs a child to stand among them. Then He states, ". . . unless you change and become like little children, you will never enter the kingdom of heaven." To change in the most basic sense means to repent. The Biblical definition of repentance means to change one's mind and heart about sin. Theologically, repentance – the turning away from sin – is linked to a corresponding turning to faith in God.[9]

Jesus further clarifies ". . . whoever humbles himself like this child is the greatest in the kingdom of heaven." Greatness in the kingdom doesn't depend on your status, education, degrees, homes, cars, money acquired, or accomplishments. The key to greatness is simply humility. To understand Jesus' instruction about humility, one must observe the character of a child. Children are open to the presence of God. They are humble, innocent, naïve, and trusting towards their parents. They are not prideful or boastful like adults may tend to act. Society teaches us that humility is a weakness of character. But God teaches us that when you are humble, you are comfortable with who you are in Jesus Christ. When you are humble, you can respond to and learn from criticism without becoming defensive.[10] Humility is an act of servanthood to others and God. The only way to be what God intends for us to be is to lay aside pride and self-promoting.

When I read this passage of scripture, the Holy Spirit reminded me of my simple lesson in humility. I never thought I struggled with pride. However, I always prided myself in the way I took care of my professional and personal business. On September 15, 2017, I was misdiagnosed and properly diagnosed with a vascular necrosis, a debilitating hip disease where there is a lack of blood flow

---

9   Vine, W. E., Merrill F. Unger, William White, Jr., *Vine's Complete Expository Dictionary of Old and New Testament*, Thomas Nelson Publishers, Nashville, 1985.

10 Britton, Doug. *The Bible Shows the Power of Humility.* Doug Britton Books, p.#21. www.dougbritton.com. Accessed August 12, 2019.

to the hip area. The only medical treatment is a total hip replacement. Unfortunately, a simple surgery on December 20, 2018, turned into a nightmare including infections, four surgeries, and one procedure. My first lesson of humility was asking my siblings to take care of me, which included moving into my home, waiting on me, helping me to bathe, and helping me put on my clothes. The only thing I could think about were my sisters seeing me naked, blemishes and all. Call me vain or whatever! However, the six-month ordeal taught me that when you are humble, you are free from pride. When you are humble, you can receive the gift of love from others and God.

During this Lenten season, what better passage of scripture to reflect upon? We are instructed to self-examine, blemishes and all. It was Socrates who supposedly said, "The unexamined life is not worth living." Lent calls us to a self-examination that reflects upon our need for God, our mortality, our sin, and how the gospel is the only answer.[11]

Prayer

Lord, "When I was a child, I talked like a child, I thought like a child, I reasoned like a child" (1 Corinthians 13:11). Let me possess a child-like faith to enter into your kingdom. Amen.

---

11 Laker, Matthew. "Beginners Guide to Lent." www.matthewlaker.com. Accessed August 12, 2019.

Reflection

Do you have a child-like trust and faith in God?

How do we practice self-examination during this Lenten season?

My Action

Meditate on Lamentations 3:40. "Let us test and examine our ways and return to the Lord!" (ESV)

March 1, 2020

First Sunday in Lent

My Personal Reflection Notes

Reflect on this past week.

What day stood out during this Lenten journey?

What did you learn about yourself and your relationship with Jesus Christ?

Which "My Action" of the week brought you great joy or struggle? Why?

Please journal your thoughts. (*Space is available on the next page for journaling.*)

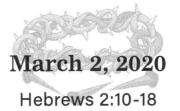

March 2, 2020
Hebrews 2:10-18

I will never forget my first year of Christmas Eve service at Wesley Chapel United Methodist Church in McDonough, Georgia. The poinsettias surrounded the altar, the choir was singing, I preached what I thought was a great sermon, families gathered from out of town, and there was an excitement in the air for commemorating the birth of Jesus. But what was strikingly different was what occurred after the benediction.

As I greeted the individuals at the end of the service and prepared to meet my family at my home, there standing in front of my office were three United Methodist Men (UMM) and one couple with tears streaming down their faces. One of my UMM shared that this couple was at the altar and the husband wanted to accept salvation. Of course, I was elated to learn that someone wanted to make a public confession of salvation.

As we all sat down in my office, the gentleman began to share that he wanted to be saved like his wife was saved. He continued to explain that he knew that Jesus Christ died for his sins and wanted to make the next steps. As I listened intently to this man's testimony,

I could only think how wonderful it felt as a young pastor to lead this man to salvation. I thought, "This is ministry!" With the support of his wife and the UMM standing with them, I asked the gentleman two questions. "First, do you acknowledge that you are a sinner?"

He answered, "Yes."

"Do you believe in your heart and confess with your mouth that Jesus Christ died for your sins and God raised Him from the dead, so that you will be saved?"

With no hesitation he answered, "Yes" again.

I glanced at his wife and she was crying, the UMM were crying, and tears were equally flowing down my face. This moment became etched in my mind and a part of my ministry to always be open to the movement of the spirit. Everyone may not make the public confession at the altar. They may be moved to come to my office. Before we left my office, there was an exchange of numbers and addresses, and the intention of a follow-up call to begin to disciple this man. Finally, I left my office with a tiredness in my spirit but a joy in my soul that someone came to Christ on Christmas Eve.

As we examine the scripture for reflection, Jesus provides the way to salvation for all of God's children. God the creator and sustainer of the universe has sent his Son to be our forerunner through his passion, death, and resurrection.[12] To do so, He became a real human being and suffered temptations as we do. However, Jesus overcame His temptations and is able to help us identify

---

12 Gaventa, Beverly Roberts and David Petersen, Editors, *The New Interpreter's Bible (One-Volume Commentary)*, Abingdon Press, Nashville, 2010, p. 883-884.

and overcome our temptations.

Jesus had to endure the ultimate suffering of the cross to make atonement for the sins of the people.[13] He chose freely to suffer for humanity and His faithfulness freed us from sin and death. As the pioneer of salvation, Christ has gone through what we go through (suffering and death) and can bring us closer to our common Father.[14] Jesus functioned as the "merciful and faithful high priest" between God and humanity.

Prayer

Lord, please allow someone to cross my path who does not have a personal relationship with you. Please use me to share my salvation experience. Amen.

---

13 Richards, p. #1069.

14 Gaventa, p.#884.

Reflection

Why did God become human?

What does it mean that Jesus Christ is the "merciful and faithful high priest"?

My Action

Memorize Romans 10:9-10. Allow the Holy Spirit to help you lead someone to Christ.

March 3, 2020

Psalm 32

Author Ernest Hemingway recounts the story of a Spanish father who took out an ad in the newspaper *El Liberal*. He wanted to be reconciled with his son who had abandoned him earlier and fled to Madrid. The ad simply read, "Paco Meet Me at Hotel Montana noon Tuesday; All is forgiven, Papa." Paco is a very common name in Spain, much like Jack is in America. When the remorseful father arrived at the square where the hotel was situated, he discovered 800 men named Paco waiting to meet their fathers. Talk about forgiveness! In fact, in the past decade, more than 200 books have been written on this topic. How many times in our lives do we stand in the need of forgiveness? How many times in our lives do we have unconfessed sins on our heart?

According to the *Nelson's Bible Dictionary*, "Forgiveness is characterized as God's pardon of the sins of human beings. Forgiveness is the act of excusing or pardoning others in spite of their shortcomings and errors."

Psalm 32, known as one of the seven traditional penitential psalms, focuses on God's forgiveness. This psalm begins with celebrating the joys of forgiveness. In verses 3-5, the psalmist recounts how unconfessed sin changes our relationship with the Lord. Sin creates turmoil in our souls. Unconfessed sin causes us to hide from God, and confession opens us up to God. When we acknowledge our sin, the Lord not only forgives us, but restores us to an intimate relationship with Him, as revealed in verses 6-7. When our sins are forgiven, we are comforted in knowing that God will protect us from trouble and surround us with His mighty power. The restored relationship makes divine instruction and counsel possible again (verses 8-10). Finally, the psalmist David is able to rejoice in the Lord (verse 11).

Prayer

Lord, my sins are forever before me. Please forgive me for being out of fellowship with you. Amen.

Reflection

Why is it hard for us to acknowledge our sin(s) before God?

Is there a fear that if we own up to our sin(s) that we will be punished?

What can we learn from the psalmist David in this passage of scripture?

My Action

Confess your sin(s) before God and ask God for forgiveness.

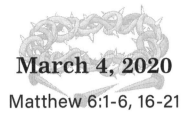

March 4, 2020
Matthew 6:1-6, 16-21

In 1999, I was appointed as the Associate Pastor of Christian Evangelism at Ben Hill United Methodist Church in Atlanta, Georgia. I was so elated to receive this appointment because in 1994 I accepted my call to ministry at Ben Hill, and later served there as the Student Minister of Children's Ministry. I was ecstatic to graduate in May, to be ordained in June, and to be appointed as an Associate Pastor.

Ben Hill was a rapidly growing African American church in the UMC connection with 8,500 members. Three worship services were held on Sunday with approximately 4,000 people in attendance, with a variety of intergenerational ministry held during the week. My foundation in ministry was developed and nurtured at Ben Hill.

My responsibilities as the Associate Pastor of Christian Evangelism were to cast a vision for the area of evangelism, discipleship, coordinate the prospect list, evangelize the community, reclaim members once a year, and teach classes for new members, confirmation, and baptism. My plate was full and the area of evangelism was constantly growing and evolving. I was glad to be appointed to an area of ministry that I was passionate about: helping people develop a relationship with Jesus Christ.

One of my responsibilities was to reclaim members to the church. This was a long and lengthy process that took patience and follow-up. First, we would digitally print out the names and addresses of members that were missing from worship. We would post these names for accuracy and ask the congregation to inquire about the whereabouts of these members. Then, we would send a letter to these folks inquiring if they were still a member of Ben Hill. Depending on the data collected, we would follow up with a call or a visit. Once a year, we would have a worship service dedicated to reclaiming members back to Ben Hill. Finally, we would make sure these members were in a Bible study, Sunday school, or small group to nurture their relationship with Jesus Christ and the church.

As I reflected on the passage for today, the shepherd and lost sheep illustration speaks of God's determination to find the lost and keep them from perishing. Jesus came into the world to save sinners and has been redeeming the lost for 2,000 years. I saw my role as the Associate Pastor of Christian Evangelism as a charge to care, love, and pursue those members who were wandering. I didn't feel that it was my role to determine if a member was a true follower of Jesus Christ. I felt it was my responsibility to find the members who had strayed away from the church and welcome them back into the fold. It is very easy for a church to turn their backs from straying members.

Straying members may bring shame and disgrace to the church. They may bring dishonor to Jesus Christ through the lifestyle of sin.

God, however, always pursues the wayward believer, and we as the body of Christ must also pursue them. We must never lose sight that everyone is important in the Kingdom of God. It is not the will of God that "one of these little ones" perish. The ninety-nine in the fold are important, but God seeks the wanderer.

Prayer

Lord, may your love for me motivate me to love and pursue those who have strayed from the Kingdom of God. Amen.

Reflection

Why does God pursue the one that strays?

What does this passage of scripture teach us about humanity?

My Action

If there is anyone in your church, Sunday school, Bible study, or small group who has been absent for a few weeks? Please call, write, or visit them.

March 5, 2020

Psalm 121

I once read that you can tell a lot about a person by where he or she looks for help in times of trouble and distress. Some people will look to their family, friends, colleagues, therapist or pastors. Life is demanding, overwhelming, and sometimes quite unbearable. I find it fascinating that our society is becoming more and more technologically advanced, but psychologists believe that as individuals we are becoming far weaker emotionally.

If we are honest with ourselves, the day-to-day hustle and grind will wear you down. In today's text, the psalmist gives us the assurance that the Lord is our helper.

As we journey together for the next several weeks, I pray that you will have confidence in knowing that there is no problem our Lord and Savior can't handle. If you are troubled about your marriage, if a loved one is facing an incurable illness, if you have experienced a rocky relationship, or you are feeling completely depleted and frustrated with your walk with God, there are hidden nuggets in this passage that can give you direction.

As we examine Psalm 121, known as a song of ascents, it is difficult to know the exact background and intent of this psalm. Some scholars believe that this and other songs of ascents found in Psalms 120-134 may have been recited by worshipers when they traveled on the road to Jerusalem to celebrate an annual religious festival. Other scholars believe that Jesus may have had this psalm in his mind when he told the parable of the Good Samaritan.

As we examine the structure of this psalm in verses 1 and 2, we are assured that God is our helper. "I lift up my eyes to the hill – where does my help come from? My help comes from the Lord, the Maker of heaven and earth."

Psalm 46:1 states, "God is our refuge and strength, a very present help in trouble." Psalm 33:20-21 states, ". . . our soul waits for the Lord; He is our help and our shield. For our heart shall rejoice in Him; because we have trusted in His holy name." "Trust is the firm belief in the honesty and reliability of another. It means to have confidence or reliance in someone or something."[15] Trust is a conscious dependence on God. Trust is found in our belief that God will indeed work on our behalf to bring God's perfect will for our lives. I know that my help comes from the Lord because I trust His Word and I trust His character.

Additionally, a word of praise to God who does not rest. "He will not let your foot slip – he who watches over you will not slumber; indeed, he who watches over Israel will neither slumber nor sleep" (verses 3 and 4). It is believed that on the journey to Jerusalem the people would have to stop and rest. Yet, they would still be cared for by God. Find confidence in this passage of scripture that our Lord will never forsake His children.

---

15 https://www.lexico.com/en/definition/trust

Third, a word of praise to God who watches His people. "The Lord watches over you – the Lord is your shade at your right hand; the sun will not harm you by day, nor the moon by night" (verses 5 and 6). The Lord is able to deal with our fears, frailties, faults, and insecurities. God is always watching and listening to our needs.

Finally, the psalmist reveals in verses 7 and 8 an affirmation that God will protect His people from daily harm. "The Lord will keep you from all harm – He will watch over your life; the Lord will watch over your coming and going both now and forevermore." John 10:10 reminds us that "Satan comes to kill, steal and destroy. But Christ came to give life and give it more abundantly."

Isn't it comforting to know that we serve a Savior who will protect us from all evil and harm? Isaiah 54:17 instructs us that "no weapons formed against you shall prosper, and every tongue, which rises against you in judgment, you shall condemn."

Prayer

Lord, I have come to know you as a helper, guardian, protector, and a shepherd that never sleeps. Amen.

Reflection

How has the Lord been a helper, guardian, and protector
in your life?

My Action

Share your testimony of the Lord being a protector in
your life.

March 6, 2020
Romans 3:21-31

S.I.N. No one likes to talk about it. No one likes to preach about it. No one likes to hold us accountable for it. However, we are sinful people and are challenged with some form of sin each day. There are seven deadly sins or vices according to Christian tradition: lust, gluttony, greed, sloth, wrath, envy, and pride. According to *Nelson Bible Dictionary*, sin is literally a "missing of the mark." St. Augustine of Hippo describes sin as a word, deed, or desire in opposition to the eternal law of God.[16] John Wesley, founder of Methodism, defines sin as a willful transgression of a known law of God.[17]

However, according to our meditation for today, "all have sinned and fall short of the glory of God." Both Jews and Gentiles have fallen short of the divine glory, but God has taken the initiative in the death of Jesus to remedy the human dilemma and to declare divine righteousness for all people.[18]

---

16 Mc Guinness, I. Sin (Theology of), in: *New Catholic Encyclopedia, vol XIII,* The Catholic University of America, Washington D.C., 1981. pp. #241-245.

17 "Catechism on Man/Sin," www.WesleyanTheology.com. http://www.wesleyantheology.com/mansin.html Question 87: "What are sins "properly so-called?" Accessed August 12, 2019.

18 Gaventa.

To understand verse 23, we must first examine its context. Verses 21-23 combine to point out that all people, without distinction, are equally deserving of wrath for our sin, and all people who are justified, without distinction, are justified through Jesus Christ.[19] As believers, being justified is the process by which sinful human beings are pardoned for our sins. Jesus Christ literally took our place on the cross.

The scripture reveals that everyone sins. Everyone has sinned. Romans 3:10 states, "There is no one righteous, not even one." The Apostle Paul clearly classifies us as sinners. "God made him who had no sin to be sin for us, so that in him we might become the righteousness of God" (2 Corinthians 5:21). Jesus Christ lived a sinless life. He chose to die on the cross and accept the punishment of our sin.

The passage of scripture indicates that not only are we sinners, "we all fall short of the glory of God." In Greek, the translation for "fall short" in the present tense means continually falling short. Because humanity has broken relational/covenantal expectations of glorifying God, we now "lack the glory of God." "Humanity has fallen short of attributing the supreme honor and glory rightly due to God."[20] To reach God's glory, the Apostle Paul reveals in verse 24 that we "are justified freely by his grace through the redemption that came by Jesus Christ." This redemption means freedom from the guilt, power, and consequences of sin.

---

19 www.BibleRef.com

20 "The Meaning of Romans 3:23," www.HonorShame.com. October 4, 2017.

I personally believe that we do not have to remain in our sins. The ongoing battle with Christians is that we want to be saved "with" our sins, instead of being saved "from" our sins. God gave us a mind to make choices every day. If you choose to continuously sin, that's your prerogative, but we must understand that with obedience comes rewards, and disobedience comes with consequences.

Prayer

Lord, I am a sinner saved by your grace through faith. Quicken my spirit to live righteously for you each day. Amen.

Reflection

How do we live a sinless life?

How do you understand the phrase "fall short of the glory of God?"

My Action

Memorize the scripture found in Luke 9:23.

March 7, 2020

Luke 7:1-10

What would happen if you had "out of the box" or crazy faith in your life? What would happen if you had absolute confidence and trust that God will come through in any situation? Would you live your life any differently? Would you live your life free of anxieties and worries?

Hebrews 11 is the model chapter on faith, illustrating many examples drawn from the Old Testament narratives. The writer of Hebrews reminds us that, "Now faith is being sure of what we hope for and certain of what we do not see" (Hebrews 11:1). The writer adds that "without faith it is impossible to please God, because anyone who comes must believe that he exists and that he rewards those who earnestly seek him."

Faith is the only currency that God accepts. Faith is reaching out for what God may throw out at you. Faith is crucial to all aspects of life. Faith is stepping into the unknown, but remembering that the God we serve is omnipotent, omniscient, and omnipresent. Faith impacts how we walk with God. Faith enables us as believers to please God. Faith means clinging to the hope that God will eventually come through in your personal situation.

The Message Bible reveals that faith is the firm foundation under everything that makes life worth living. It's our handle on what we can't see. The Contemporary English Bible reveals that faith makes us sure of what we hope for and gives us proof of what we cannot see. Faith is so essential to our being that in the African American Church we have a song to encourage our spiritual journey, titled, "We've Come This Far by Faith."

We've come this far by faith
Leaning on the Lord
Trusting in His Holy Word
He never failed me yet
Oh, oh, oh, oh, oh, oh
No turning around
We've come this far by faith.[21]

As we reflect on today's meditation, "faith" is a topic that runs strongly through both of Luke's writings: the Gospel of Luke and the Book of Acts. Luke introduced a Gentile – a centurion – who demonstrated "great faith" by expressing the conviction that Jesus was able to heal his critically ill servant by simply speaking a word – from a distance![22]

There are several lessons we can learn from the centurion officers. First, the centurion was unashamed to approach Jesus. He knew that he was not worthy to have

---

21 McClurkin, Donnie. "We've Come This Far by Faith." 2004.

22 Richards.

Jesus enter his house. However, he had heard about Jesus' miraculously healing power: healing the man born blind, the woman with the issue of blood, and the paralytic. The centurion who had "great faith" represented all Gentiles who had learned to have faith and trust in Jesus.

Secondly, the centurion was unselfish. The centurion officer, who supervised a hundred soldiers, focused primarily on the need of his servant. The healing of his servant took top priority over commanding his soldiers.

Thirdly, the centurion was unassuming in his posture. His attitude and appeal were dressed with the characteristic of humility. The state of being humble will carry you a long way in life. He knew that to host Jesus in his house could tarnish the reputation of Jesus Christ. Lastly, the centurion's faith was unrelenting. He believed that the Lord could speak the servant's healing from afar; Jesus Christ's physical presence was not required, just His word. We must come to understand on this journey that God's Word is enough.

Prayer

Lord, give me the stamina and the unrelenting faith to believe in your healing even from afar. Amen.

Reflection

How do we build our faith?

Can you believe God when you have no physical evidence?

Do we believe that healing miracles do occur?

My Action

Do an online search for "healing stories" and read or listen to someone's testimony.

March 8, 2020

Second Sunday in Lent

My Personal Reflection Notes

Reflect on this past week.

What day stood out during this Lenten journey?

What did you learn about yourself and your relationship with Jesus Christ?

Which "My Action" of the week brought you great joy or struggle?

Why?

Please journal your thoughts. (*Space is available on the next page for journaling.*)

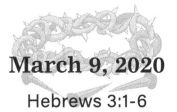

March 9, 2020
Hebrews 3:1-6

*Jesus, Jesus, Jesus; there just something about
that name.*

Master, Savior, Jesus, like the fragrance after the rain,

Jesus, Jesus, Jesus, let all Heaven and earth proclaim

Kings and kingdoms will all pass away...

But there's something about that name [23]

Before reading the rest of the reflection, please listen
to "There's Something About that Name" by the Gaithers.
It is on YouTube.com. (See footnote below.) Every time
I hear this song, whether on the radio, at church, or at
a conference, it resonates in my spirit with the love and
beauty of Jesus Christ. Philippians 2:10-11 reminds us
"that at the name of Jesus every knee shall bow, in heaven
and on earth and under the earth, and every tongue
confess that Jesus Christ is Lord."

As we reflect on the mediation for today's lesson, the

23 Gaither, Gloria, and William Gaither. "There's Something About that Name." 1970. Gaither
Music TV. https://www.youtube.com/watch?v=cwzP1jiYhi0. Accessed August 9, 2019.

Hebrew writer is making a statement that Jesus Christ is greater than Moses, the law-giver. The comparison with Moses is designed not to disparage Moses, but rather to affirm the authority of the Son in his status. Both are distinguished for their faithfulness to God. But Moses was faithful as a servant in God's household, whereas Christ is faithful as the Son of God who presides over God's household. [24]

Do we know that Jesus Christ is the Son of the Living God? Unfortunately, I have experienced that the twenty-first century church is afraid to acknowledge or confess the lordship of Jesus Christ. In the church, we fall prey to watering down the gospel and the name of Jesus in an attempt to not offend people or other religions. What I don't understand is that we confess that we are Christians, we wear crosses around our necks, we worship on Sunday with lifted holy hands, but when we are asked to witness about our Savior, we are timid. As believers, why don't we stand for Jesus and the teachings of Jesus?

In the Methodist Church, we sing a hymn: "Standing on the promises of Christ my king, through eternal ages let his praises ring. Glory in the highest, I will shout and sing. I'm standing on the promises of God."[25] As people of God, will we be able to stand in the midst of adversity in our lives? Will we be able to stand in our churches and reclaim our youth? Will we be able to stand against the mass incarceration that is on the rise? Will we be able to stand and speak truth to power? Will we be able to proclaim with

---

24 Gaventa.

25 Carter, Russell Kelso. "Standing on the Promises." 1886.

boldness and authority that Jesus Christ is the Son of God, Lord of Creations, and Savior of the World?

First, what God asks of us is that we come to know Jesus. Not knowing *about* Jesus, but knowing Jesus personally for ourselves. It is imperative that we strive to have a one-on-one relationship with the Master. It is very easy to have head knowledge only. But when you have a personal relationship with Jesus Christ, the knowledge of Christ moves from your head to your heart, and then your life will be transformed.

Secondly, we must proclaim Him as the Messiah in our own lives. To "proclaim" is characterized as to "declare formally." *Messiah* is a Hebrew word that means "anointed one." It is the equivalent of the New Testament word *Christ* which also means "anointed." As the Messiah, Christ has delivered us from the bonds of sin and death. A confession about our salvation in Jesus is stated in Romans 10:9, "that if you confess with your mouth, 'Jesus is Lord,' and believe in your heart that God raised him from the dead, you will be saved."

Finally, what God asks of us is to share the Good News. Share the Good News of the teachings of Jesus Christ. Share the gospel message that God loved us so much that God sent His Only Son to die on the cross to reconcile us back to God. Jesus Christ commanded the apostles in Acts 1:8b: "and you will be my witnesses in Jerusalem, and in all Judea and Samaria and to the ends of the earth."

Prayer

Lord, I confess that I know you are my Lord and Savior and you died on the cross for my sins. Amen.

Reflection

Why are we afraid to witness about the beauty of our Lord and Savior Jesus Christ?

My Action

Please share how you have come to know Jesus as your personal Lord and Savior with someone this week.

March 10, 2020
Isaiah 65:17-25

One of the hardest things I've had to do as a minister is to preach my sister, Wanda Hendrix's, eulogy. But the passage of scripture for today's reflection brought me great strength and comfort as we prepared her visitation and funeral. Isaiah 65:17-18 states, "Behold, I will create new heavens and a new earth. The former things will not be remembered nor will they come to mind. But be glad and rejoice forever in what I will create, for I will create Jerusalem to be a delight and its people a joy."

On November 11, 2013, Wanda was scheduled for a hysterectomy. I remember praying with her before surgery that God would guide the hands of the doctors and she would no longer suffer from the piercing pain. Unfortunately, a two-hour surgery lasted longer because Wanda had an emergency appendectomy. There were several ups and downs after surgery. I will never forget the call from my brother-in-law, Bernard, instructing me to come to the hospital because Wanda had taken a turn for the worse. As I hastily drove to the hospital, I remember praying fervently for God to spare my sister's life. When I reached the hospital, I was instructed by a nurse to go to one of the rooms down the hall. Wanda was lying in the bed in excruciating pain and Bernard had a look of frustration and fear that we might lose her. As I tried to be encouraging, to my dismay, she asked me to help her plan her funeral. I said, "No! We are going to fight 'this.'" She persisted and uttered these words, "Y'all know I'm not afraid to die." Holding back the tears, I reached for a pad that was in the room and we sat and planned her funeral to the minute details. The scriptures she wanted read or preached, the songs she wanted sung by her choir (Majestic Choir), who she wanted to share remarks, and how she wanted her hair parted on the side. On February 13, 2014, she entered into eternal rest. Wanda – a vibrant woman, mother, and sister – died from complications from surgery.

As I helped my brother-in-law prepare for the funeral and to be sensitive to what Wanda requested, this text in Isaiah 65:17-25 paralleled Revelation 21:1-5. "Then I saw a new heaven and a new earth, for the first heaven and the first earth had passed away and there was no longer any sea. I saw the Holy City, the new Jerusalem coming down out of heaven from God . . . ."

In the new heaven and earth, God will eradicate all anguish revealed in Revelation 7:16, "Never again will they hunger; never again will they thirst." Both scriptures in Isaiah and Revelation bring comfort, because out of the new heaven comes a new city, the eternal rest of the redeemed, where God lives with His saints.[26] Newness means total liberation from the bondage of sin and death. According to scholars, heaven will erase five aspects of

---

26 *Disciple's Study Bible,* New International Version, Holman Bible Publishers, Nashville, p.#1655.

the human experience: tears, death, mourning, crying, and pain. As we celebrated Wanda's life, I found comfort knowing that in her eternal resting place she would experience no more tears, death, mourning, crying or pain. My life was forever changed. Wanda was my first sibling to pass. Her brief illness taught me the importance of family support, that life was unpredictable, and the power of prayer. Prayer to sustain you. Prayer to give you strength. Prayer to bring you comfort.

Prayer

Lord, when we are faced with the death of our loved ones, let us find comfort in knowing that you have prepared a Holy City, a new Jerusalem. Amen.

Reflection

How do you imagine the Holy City, a new Jerusalem?

What scriptures bring you comfort during death?

My Action

At the next memorial or funeral, pay close attention to the scriptures that are used in worship to bring comfort to bereaved family and friends.

March 11, 2020
John 7:53-8:11

This story has always been intriguing to me as a pastor and continues to depict the double standards between women and men. Unfortunately, in 2020 what is frightening is that women are still plagued with the injustices of sexual misconduct and misogyny. When facing sexual misconduct, a woman's life and sexual promiscuity is called into question. She is scrutinized in order to deduce if she is telling the truth, and the man involved is treated very differently and never really called into question. When facing misogyny, the woman is faced with the dislike or contempt of prejudicial behavior. The mere fact that she is a woman puts her at a disadvantage in many areas.

As the story unfolds, this nameless woman caught in adultery was brought into the temple courts to stand in front of this group. The teachers of the law and the Pharisees knew without a shadow of a doubt they had Jesus caught between a rock and a hard place. If Jesus said, "Stone her," He would probably ruin His reputation. If He said, "Let her go," He would have been in violation of Moses' Law. Interestingly, where would you go to catch a woman in the act of adultery? Who was the man? Why did they let the man go? These questions have always been a source of conversation for me.

Some scholars believe that when Jesus wrote on the ground, He recorded the sins of the men present. Remarkably, they left the scene one by one, afraid they would be exposed. Whether or not this is the case, it is dangerous to condemn others. When we condemn others, we are condemning ourselves. The Apostle Paul reminds us in Romans 3:23, "for all have sinned and fall short of the glory of God."

What's shocking in this passage of scripture is Jesus' words, "'Woman, where are they? Has no one condemned you?' 'No one, sir,' she said. 'Then neither do I condemn you,' Jesus declared."

Then Jesus said, "Go now and leave your life of sin." This conversation confirms what John writes in 3:17, "For God did not send his Son into the world to condemn the world, but to save the world through him." John 3:16-17 captures the role of Jesus. That God loved us so much that He sent His only son to save us and not to condemn us, with the assurance that we would be reconciled back to God.

What is powerful about this conversation is that Jesus' encounter sets in motion her new life: "Go now and leave your life of sin." He did not ask her any questions or sit and have a discussion or debate about her present condition. He simply states, ". . . leave your life of sin." I truly believe that when you have an encounter with the Master your life is forever changed.

I remember my parents telling me the story of my first

encounter with the Lord. I was baptized at six months old, at Brannen Chapel United Methodist Church in Statesboro, Georgia. Actually, that encounter was my parents' encounter. However, what I do remember is at the young age of twelve, I encountered the Lord Jesus one Sunday morning at Brannen Chapel, and my life and destiny changed forever. I sat next to my dad because my mom normally ushered every Sunday. The older adult choir was singing a hymn as well as they could, and Rev. George Bradley was near the end of his sermon. I remember Rev. Bradley walking down from the pulpit and standing in front of the altar rail. As usual, he extended his hand for an invitation to join the church and an invitation to Christian discipleship. The only thing I recall is that my legs carried me forward and I was standing in front of Rev. Bradley ready to make a personal commitment to Jesus Christ. I believe this encounter began my Christian journey and my call into ministry. We never know in life where the encounter with the Master will lead us.

Prayer

Lord, please forgive me all the times we have judged women wrongly. Let me not tear down women, but build them up and be an advocate for women's issues. Amen.

Reflection

Who was the man and why did they let him go?

Why does society continue to marginalize women as second-class citizens? What will it take for women to take their rightful place in the justice system?

My Action

Volunteer at a battered women's shelter or rape crisis center. As men may not be able to volunteer, perhaps donating or organizing the collection of hygiene kits to be given to women's shelters, a rape crisis center, or a women's prison would be possible.

March 12, 2020

Exodus 16:1-8

As we examine our passage of scripture for today, we can trust God to supply our needs. Proverbs 3:5-6 states, "Trust in the Lord with all your heart and lean not to your own understanding. In all your ways acknowledge Him, and He will direct your path." *The Message Bible* states, "Trust God from the bottom of your heart; don't try to figure out everything on your own. Listen for God's voice in everything you do, everywhere you go. He's the one who will keep you on track."

I was once told a story of a man who was out jogging one day. As he passed a cliff, he got too close and fell. Grabbing hold to a branch, he was stranded. No way up and certainly no way down. He of course began to scream, "Help! Is anyone up there who can hear me?" He yelled for hours, and was about to give up when he heard a voice.

"Can you hear me?"

"Yes, yes I can hear you. I'm down here."

"I can see you, are you all right?"

"Yes, but who are you and where are you?"

"I am the Lord; I am everywhere."

"'The Lord?' You mean God?"

"That's me."

"God, help me! I promise that if you get me down from here, I'll stop sinning, I will pay my tithes, and I will go to Bible study. I'll be a really good person and serve you the rest of my life."

The Lord replied, "Easy on the promises. First, let's get you down, then we can discuss those promises."

The man replied in desperation, "I'll do anything, just tell me what to do."

The Lord replied, "Okay, let go of the branch."

The man replied, "What?!"

"I said, 'Let go of the branch.' Just TRUST me and let go."

PAUSE.

The man replied, "Help, Help! Is there anybody else up there?"

Trusting God is probably one of the hardest spiritual disciplines to accomplish. As our story unfolds, the Israelites had come out of Egypt. The passage of scripture reveals that in the desert, the whole community begins to grumble against Moses and Aaron about food scarcity. The Israelites complained, "If only we had died by the Lord's hand in Egypt. There we sat around pots of meat and ate all the food we wanted, but you have brought us out into this desert to starve this assembly to death" (Exodus 16:3).

The first lesson of the Israelites is that they had to learn to trust God beyond what they understood and comprehended. They could not believe that Moses and Aaron had directed them to the desert to die when Egypt had an abundance of food. It is God's will for us to trust God with everything. It was not enough that God had delivered them out of Pharaoh's hand.

Then the Lord tells Moses, "I will rain down bread from heaven for you." He instructed Moses that the Israelites are to go and gather enough food for each day. "On the sixth day, the Israelites are to prepare what they bring in, and that is to be twice as much as they gather on the other days" (Exodus 16: 4-5). The second lesson of the Israelites was that the Lord has unlimited resources. We are reminded in 1 Chronicles 29:11 that ". . . everything in the heavens and earth is yours, O Lord, and this is your kingdom. We adore you as the one who is over all things."

Finally, Moses and Aaron reassure the Israelites that they will know it was the Lord who brought them out of Egypt, because meat and bread will be provided for them, despite their grumbling. The third lesson of the Israelites was God will always supply your needs. Philippians 4:19 affirms, "And my God will meet all your needs according to his glorious riches in Christ Jesus."

Prayer

Lord, help me to totally trust in your will and your ways. I know your Word confirms that "you shall supply all my needs according to the riches and glory in Christ Jesus." Amen.

Reflection

Why is trusting God so hard? How does our faith factor into trusting God?

Why was it hard for the Israelites to believe that God will make the provisions for them?

My Action

Provide an unexpected meal for a friend, co-worker, or family member.

March 13, 2020
Exodus 16:9-21

Do we believe that miracles can exist in 2020? Or do we believe in luck? Albert Einstein said, "There are only two ways to live your life. One is as if nothing is a miracle. The other is as if everything is a miracle."

The *Nelson Bible Dictionary* describes a miracle as "a historical event or natural phenomena that appears to violate natural laws." I believe that miracles are happening all around us, but we have ceased to believe in God's supernatural power. As a result, we serve a God who can never surprise us, never overwhelm us, never astonish us, and never transcend us.

A valuable way of understanding the meaning of miracles is to examine the various terms for miracles used in the Bible. Both the Old and New Testament use the word "sign," found in Isaiah 7:11, 14 and John 2:11 to denote a miracle that points to a deeper revelation. The word "wonder" is often used to emphasize the effect of the miracle, causing awe, and even terror. The term "work" points to the presence of God in history, acting on the behalf of humankind. The New Testament uses the word "power" to emphasize God's acting in strength. You will notice that these terms often overlap in meaning.

When we examine miracles in the Old Testament, the readers recognize that God is the Creator and Sustainer of all life. This assumption permitted the Israelites to comprehend the possibility of miracles. The miracles were not so much a proof for God's existence but a revelation of the faithfulness of God's covenant love. To prove this point, when God parted the Red Sea or when God saved Israel in Egypt through the Passover, God revealed His character and the Israelites were convinced that God was working for their salvation. Miracles were characterized as expressions of God's saving love as well as God's holy justice. In addition, miracles were connected with great events in Israel's history.

The New Testament miracles are simply expressions of God's salvation and glory. Why did Jesus perform miracles? In the New Testament, the theme of miracles pointing to the Kingdom of God was developed in the Gospel of John. John presented the miracles of Jesus as "signs" on seven different occasions. He thought of these miracles as pointing to "deep spiritual truth" demanding obedient faith. In the New Testament, every miracle story was a sign that God's salvation was present.

As I began this reflection, I asked the question, "How many of you believe that miracles still exist today?" I want to remind you as the reader that God's love and power is not limited by the human imagination.

There is a song that we sing in the African American Church, "Expect a Miracle."

I expect a miracle everyday
God can make a way, out of no way
Just believe and receive. God can perform it
today.[27]

In verses 11-12, the Lord said to Moses, "I have heard
the grumbling of the Israelites. 'Tell them, at twilight you
will eat meat, and in the morning you will be filled with
bread. Then you will know that I am the Lord your God.'"
There are more than 37,000 promises in the Bible. God did
not have to promise anything to sinful people. The mere
fact that almost all Biblical promises are those made by
God to human beings indicates that His nature is characterized by grace and faithfulness. In verses 15-16, Moses
said to them, "It is the bread the Lord has given you to
eat. This is what the Lord has commanded: each one is
to gather as much as he needs. Take an omer[28] for each
person you have in your tent."

Prayer

Lord, give me eyes to see and the faith to believe that
miracles are happening every day. Amen.

---

27 The Clark Sisters. "Expect a Miracle." Miracle. Sparrow, 1994.

28 The omer (Hebrew: עֹמֶר 'ōmer) is an ancient Israelite unit of dry measure used in the era of
the Temple in Jerusalem. It is used in the Bible as an ancient unit of volume for grains and dry
commodities, and the Torah mentions it as being equal to one tenth of an ephah.

Reflection

Why did the Israelites still not believe that food was going to be provided?

Once food had been provided, why did they still save it and not believe there would be more?

My Action

Read or listen to the testimony of Mrs. Gertrude Ticer's miracle. [29] Pray with someone who is desiring a miracle in their life.

---

29 Available on YouTube at https://www.youtube.com/watch?v=LMyzG1Jdo2l as of September 15, 2019.

March 14, 2020

John 4:1-6

In this week's text, I'm reminded of the importance of personal evangelism. One may ask, "What is evangelism?" Growing up in small town Statesboro, I thought evangelizing was knocking on doors on Saturday mornings like the Jehovah Witnesses. One simple definition is that evangelism is "sharing the gospel message with those who are not believers." Or in an older definition, evangelism has been described as one beggar telling another beggar where to find bread.[30] According to George Barna, the average Christian comes into contact with seven unchurched people daily. This figure is startling to me, because I realize how many times I've probably missed the opportunity to share Jesus Christ assuming that people are saved. On an average day, with whom are we coming into contact: coworkers, the mailman, fitness trainers, servers, grocery cashiers, family, and friends?

John sets up this narrative as Jesus travels from Judea to Galilee to Sychar. Tired from his journey and sitting by the well, Jesus encounters a Samaritan woman during the

---

30 D.T. Niles is credited with this saying.

sixth hour. Interestingly, the Samaritan woman was disregarded by the other women who would draw water from the well. The lack of communication from the other women was rare because drawing water at the community well was a time for socializing. Could it be that the Samaritan woman was considered an outsider in her own community?

The Samaritan woman was considered an outcast in the Jewish social system. First, she was from a mixed ethnic lineage and her marital status was in question. In addition, a Jewish rabbi was never allowed to talk with a woman without her husband present. The Jewish social system would consider her unclean, and a Jewish person would feel contaminated if they interacted with her.

However, what we witness in the text is that no social barrier was too extreme for the gospel message to cross. Jesus demonstrated through His actions that the Samaritan woman had worth and value. He was determined to lead her to faith. Jesus reminded his apostles in Acts 1:8b: ". . . and you will be my witnesses in Jerusalem, and in all Judea and Samaria, and to the ends of the earth." In her day, the Samaritan woman was seen as an outcast, a mixed-breed person, and a minority, and was treated as such. Unfortunately, in today's society we are still plagued by, and fighting against, racial and social injustices against minority races.

According to scholars, only in John's Gospel do we see that Jesus was involved in ministry in Judea during the same time as John the Baptist. However, John is very clear to convey to the readers that Jesus' disciples were baptizing in Judea. The Pharisees therefore forced him to leave and return to Galilee and then to Samaria.

John gives us the practices for personal evangelism in the Lord's dialogue with the woman of Samaria by conveying that a witness: (1) is concerned with one individual, (2) begins with felt needs and desires of the lost person, (3) directs the conversation to the person's basic spiritual need, (4) shows the person his or her sin and the need of salvation, (5) keeps the conversation from straying from the real issue, (6) points to Jesus as the Savior, and (7) leads the new convert to witness to others.[31] In 2020, do we care about the salvation of our brothers and sisters in Christ? Do we have a hunger to lead people to the faith?

Prayer

Lord, give me the hunger and the desire to witness my faith to an unbeliever. Amen.

Reflection

How important is it for us to witness to the unbeliever?

Who is your Samaritan woman or man?

---

31 *Disciple Bible Study Notes.*

My Action

Invite an unbeliever to a worship service. Commit to praying for his or her salvation.

March 15, 2020

Third Sunday in Lent

My Personal Reflection Notes

Reflect on this past week.

What day stood out during this Lenten journey?

What did you learn about yourself and your relationship with Jesus Christ?

Which "My Action" of the week brought you great joy or struggle? Why?

Please journal your thoughts. (*Space is available on the next page for journaling.*)

March 16, 2020
2 John 1:1-13

L-O-V-E has been described as a strong affection for another arising out of kinship or personal ties. Love can be described as an intense emotional attachment for a pet or treasured object. The concept of love has inspired some of the world's best and worst poetry, songs, television shows, and movies. For example, "How Do I Love Thee" by Elizabeth Barrett Brown, "I Will Always Love You" by Whitney Houston, *Bachelor/Bachelorette*, and *The Notebook*.

The Bible teaches us that "Love covers the multitude of sins, that perfect love casts out fear, to love your enemies, and to pray for those who persecute you." Love is the foundation of the Christian faith and theology. It refers to the love of Jesus Christ for humanity, the love of Christians for Christ, and the love of Christians for others (John 15:9-17).

The theme of love is the central element in the Johannine writings. This is demonstrated in one of the most widely quoted scriptures in the Bible, John 3:16 (KJV): "For God so loved the world, that he gave his only begotten Son, that whosoever believeth in him should not perish but have everlasting life." Near the end of the Last Supper, Jesus gives His disciples "a new commandment: love one another, as I have loved you . . . By this shall all men know that you are my disciples" (John 13:34-45).

In today's text, there can never be too many prompts to love and keep Jesus' commandments. John 14:15 states, "If you love me, keep my commandments." In Mark 12:31 he says, "The second is this: 'love your neighbor as yourself.' There is no commandment greater than these." John emphasized a particular reality all Christians are to experience: that we show our obedience to Jesus, and our harmony with Him, by loving fellow believers.[32] Christians are bound together through their mutual love, which is a reflection of their love for Christ.[33]

In 2018-2019, I experienced the ultimate love of Jesus Christ from my brothers and sisters in the UMC connection and the world. Unfortunately, I have had four hip surgeries to correct a condition called a vascular necrosis or osteonecrosis. This disease causes a decrease in the blood supply to the bone, which leads to bone cell death. The surgeries led to two infections and limited mobility, which forced me to ask for medical leave for six months.

When the doctor ordered this leave, I thought I was going to lose my mind. I couldn't remember the last time that I was not employed by some company or the UMC. However, what helped me through this ordeal was the constant prayers and the expressions of love that came in the gifts of prayer blankets, flowers, plants, books, Facebook posts, cards, emails, texts, food, and phone

---

32 Richards, passim.

33 Barclay, William. *The Gospel of John: The New Daily Study Bible*, Vol 2, 2001. p #197.

calls. As I reflect, there was never a day that the love of
Jesus Christ was not shown to me and my family. I will
always be humbly appreciative and grateful for the love
that blessed my life and ministry during my recovery.
I have always believed that if you genuinely love God's
people, they will reciprocate the love back.

Love Works...

A guardian angel
Flew down from above,
To teach me a lesson
About the powers of love.
She whispers to me,
Take a hold of my hand,
There are so many things
I wish you to understand.
About the powers of love,
And all it can do,
To someone who needs
To share it with you.
A pat on the back,
A kind smile on your face
Can make someone's life
A much brighter place
It doesn't take much,
To show someone you care,
To give them the love,
God gave you to share.
So please keep in mind,
All the powers you possess,

To grace someone's life
When they're in distress.
You've been put on this earth
To bestow the powers of love,
And with those final words,
She disappeared up above.

Author Unknown

Prayer

Lord, help me to love my neighbor as I love you. Amen.

Reflection

Why is it important to show the love of Jesus Christ to our neighbors?

How do you love the unlovable?

My Action

Show the love of Jesus Christ by inviting your neighbor out to breakfast, lunch, or dinner.

March 17, 2020
Psalm 81

In today's society, the word "obedience" has little meaning. No one likes to follow rules or directions! Our natural instinct is to protest. No one likes to be told what to do. For example, if a minister mentioned the word "obey" in the wedding vows, there would be a silent uproar or no wedding. We like to control our own situation and destiny. Growing up in Statesboro, Georgia, respecting your elders was never called into question. And if you attempted not to respect your elders, there was a price to pay when you got home. It was expected in the neighborhood that before you would step into the house, your attitude or bad behavior had already been reported by a family member, friend, or even a teacher.

I was always astonished how my mother knew what happened in school and on the school bus. Currently, if anyone attempted to call your home and report on the behavior of your child, the modern-day parent would be outraged.

The word "obey" in the twenty-first century has come to have a negative connotation. The English translation means to "do as you are told, comply with, follow the commands, or to follow the direction of another."[34] Obedience is characterized as an inward reverence with an outward expression. Dietrich Bonhoeffer states, "You can only learn what obedience is by obeying." Obedience can be costly and difficult. But whether you are a child or an adult, ironically, we have a problem with the word "obey."

However, in this world you will obey something or someone. For example:

- If you want to drive and maintain your license and insurance – you must be obedient to the speed limit.

- If you want to eat and dine in a nice restaurant – you must be obedient to the dress code.

- If you want to maintain your job and lifestyle – you must be obedient to your employer.

- If you want to have a productive and fulfilled life – you must be obedient to God's Word.

In today's reading, the psalmist opens up the text with a call to praise and the words of God, which were probably spoken by a priest or temple leader.[35] Verses 3-5 capture the psalm's location at the Festival of Tabernacles, Israel's fall harvest. In verses 6-16, God is speaking through the priest and reminding the Israelites to listen and obey the voice of God. The call to obey the Lord is driven by the reminder of God's loving action for the people and God's promise to care for the people.[36] God

34 https://www.merriam-webster.com/dictionary/obey

35 Gaventa, p. #332.

36 Ibid.

speaking through the psalmist, said, "If my people would but listen to me, if Israel would follow my ways, how quickly would I subdue their enemies and turn my hands against their foes" (Psalm 81:13). This psalm indicates that God is always willing to bless and protect. It was Israel's own failure to listen to the Lord and submit to Him that led to disaster.[37]

Why is it so hard for humanity to be obedient to the Word of God? If we truly believe that the Lord is the Creator, why is obedience to God's Word so hard to practice? What does that say about your ability to trust God for the outcome? Is our unwillingness to be obedient to the Word of God keeping us from the blessings of God?

Prayer

Lord, obedience is difficult for me. Help me to be obedient to your Word. Amen.

Reflection

Read 1 Samuel 15:22 in the NIV translation. Reflect on "Obedience is better than sacrifice." How is this scripture relevant to your life?

---

37 Richards, p. #352.

Read Acts 5:29 in the NIV translation. Reflect on "We must obey God rather than men." How is this scripture relevant to your life?

My Action

Read the story of Noah and reflect on Noah's actions of obedience.

March 18, 2020

John 7:14-31, 37-39

It is amazing to me that in 2020 people are still uncertain about the existence of Jesus Christ. Who was Jesus Christ? According to the scripture, in Philippians 2:8, "and being found in human form, He humbled himself by becoming obedient to the point of death, even death on the cross." First Peter 2:2 states, "He committed no sin, and no deceit was found in His mouth." And John 8:42 states, "Jesus said, 'If God were your Father, you would love me, for I came from God and now am here. I have not come on my own, but He sent me.'"

Have you ever stopped to think who is Jesus Christ to you? (Take a few moments now and reflect on the question—*Who is Jesus Christ to me?*) Would words like "Savior," "Healer," "Deliverer," "Wonderful Counselor," "Mighty God," "Prince of Peace," "Rose of Sharon," "Paraclete," "El Elyon," "Jehovah Jireh," and "Jehovah Shalom" come to your mind? Through the years, novels, stories, television documentaries, and movies have been written about the life, ministry, and teachings of Jesus Christ. Debates may have occurred about who Jesus Christ is, but no one denies that Jesus Christ changed the course of history.

In today's reading, the same uncertainty of Jesus Christ was prevalent 2,000 years ago. Jesus goes to the Feast of Tabernacles to teach in the temple courts where gossip about Him was discussed. The text reveals that "Among the crowds there was widespread whispering about him. Some said, 'He is a good man'" (John 7:12). His teaching at the temple was called into question because his knowledge and credentials did not suffice the Jewish leaders. Jesus' teaching astonished the people. He was not looking for honor, but wanted to bring truth and honor to God. The Jewish leaders took great satisfaction in their knowledge of scripture and wanted to kill Jesus because He was feigning to be the Messiah. Jesus clarified that he received his teaching directly from "the One who sent Me" (John 8:29). This was a dual claim: to have been "sent" from God meant to speak with His authority. To have been taught by Him meant that Jesus was a channel of revelation![38]

Not only did they question His credentials and what He was teaching, they debated His true identity. "On the last and greatest day of the Feast Jesus stood and said in a loud voice, 'If anyone is thirsty let him come to me and drink. Whoever believes in me as the Scripture has said streams of living water will flow from within him'" (John 7:37). In the midst of the uncertainty, Jesus reveals Himself as the giver of living water, calling people to come and drink. The author makes it clear that water is symbolic of the Spirit. Thus, by offering living water, Jesus draws the festival to himself, revealing His giving of the Spirit as the promised gift of water flowing

---

38 Richards, p. #776.

sumptuously from the Temple in the last days revealed in Zechariah 14:8.[39]

Prayer

Lord, I open my heart to know you and your teachings. Amen.

Reflection

Do you have a personal relationship with Jesus Christ?

Has your relationship with Jesus Christ been strengthened during this Lenten season?

39 Gaventa, p. #720.

My Action

If you are an unbeliever and desire salvation, please pray the prayer below.

Dear God, I know I'm a sinner, and I ask for your forgiveness. I believe Jesus Christ is Your Son. I believe that He died for my sin and that you raised Him to life. I want to trust Him as my Savior and follow Him as Lord, from this day forward. Guide my life and help me to do your will. I pray this in the name of Jesus. Amen. [40]

---

40 Billy Graham Evangelistic Association. www.PeaceWithGod.net. Accessed August 12, 2019.

March 19, 2020

Ephesians 4:25-32

Have you ever been so hurt that you did not feel like forgiving because the pain or disappointment felt so real? Have you ever been so angry you did not feel like forgiving because the anger over the situation got in the way of your rational thinking and reasoning? Have you ever been so discouraged that you did not want to forgive because there was a violation of trust in the relationship?

As Christians, how do we deal with these feelings? How do we rise above the hurt, the pain, the anger, or the betrayal inflicted upon us by a friend, family member, spouse, or even a church member?

In our reflection today, the Apostle Paul states, "Be kind and compassionate to one another, forgiving each other, just as in Christ God forgave you."

According to the *Nelson's Bible Dictionary*, "Forgiveness is the act of excusing or pardoning others in spite of their shortcomings and errors." Forgiveness is a gracious response to having been wronged by another.

Professor Kenneth J. Collins states, "We must understand that forgiveness may not lead to reconciliation or even contact, for perpetrators may desire no such thing, but it can lead to significant physical, emotional and spiritual healing for the forgiver, as several studies have shown."[41] According to some researchers, forgiveness involves "rooting out one's negative thoughts, feelings and behaviors directed at an offender and developing positive thoughts, feelings and behaviors towards him or her."[42]

In this epistle, the Apostle Paul is writing to the Ephesians during his imprisonment in Rome. Paul is holding a mirror for us to examine ourselves. "Put off falsehood and speak truthfully, do not let the sun go down while you are angry and do not give the devil a foothold." He challenges us to no longer steal and be careful what words come out of our mouths. Instead of bitterness, rage, and slander, allow kindness, compassion, and forgiveness for one another.

As believers we must continue to practice the spirit of forgiveness. God's forgiveness of us requires that we forgive others because grace brings responsibility and obligation. Luke 6:37 states, "Do not judge, and you will not be judged. Do not condemn, and you will not be condemned. Forgive, and you will be forgiven." As Christians, we are required to forgive those who sin against us. The Lord's Prayer reveals, "And forgive us our debts, as we also have forgiven our debtors." "But if you do not forgive others their sins, your Father will not forgive

---

41 Collins, Kenneth J. *The Theology of John Wesley: Holy Love and the Shape of Grace,* Abingdon Press, Nashville, 2007.

42 Ibid.

your sins" (Matthew 6:15). How do we expect our Lord and Savior to forgive us if we can't forgive our neighbors? Can we forgive?

Forgiveness is not overlooking the hurt that comes from a weak sense of self. Any relationship in which forgiveness is not essential is a shallow relationship. South African Archbishop Desmond Tutu captured just how vital forgiveness is for relationships when he stated, "Without forgiveness there is no future."

Christ placed no limits on the extent to which we are to forgive others. Matthew writes in Chapter 18:21-22, "Then Peter came to Jesus and asked, 'Lord, how many times shall I forgive my brother or sister who sins against me? Up to seven times?' Jesus answered, 'I tell you, not seven times, but seventy-seven times.'" Can you forgive?

Prayer

Lord, please allow me to forgive myself, so I will be able to forgive others. Amen.

Reflection

Is there anyone in my present or past that I need to forgive?

Is there any unforgiveness that I thought I was healed completely from, but this devotional has caused me to reflect?

My Action

If there is anyone in your family, church, or workplace that you need to forgive, please make the effort in this season to make amends.

March 20, 2020

Ephesians 5:1-9

Several years ago, during a clergy executive session at the North Georgia Annual Conference, the Chairperson of the Order of Elders shared receiving an email from another pastor. It was concerning the Order of Elders quarterly meeting. (When we are ordained Elders, we become a part of the Order of Elders. The Order of Elders meets for spiritual formation and fellowship.) However, when the email was sent, there was a mistake in the typing and the email read the "Odor of Elders." Of course, you could hear the laughter among the colleagues.

Interestingly, the Chair raised several questions. Do we have an odor? Is our odor a sweet smell in God's nostrils? He challenged us by commenting, "Many of us needed to get rid of our existing odor of envy, jealousy, backbiting, nonsupport of each other, and the odor of competition for the better appointment." As a token of his love toward the rest of the Elders, he gave each of us a sample of deodorant. I must admit that this state-ment of the "Odor of Elders" pricked my conscience. I realized that not only can clergy have an odor problem, but the church (the body of Christ) can have similar odor problems, like gossiping, backbiting, and exclusion.

An odor can be characterized as a quality of something that stimulates the olfactory organ, or it can be characterized simply as a smell. An odor can be pleasant, like the cooking of a sweet potato pie or the aroma of Starbucks coffee. But an odor can also be pungent, distracting, and rotten, like week-old garbage. I believe that we can suffer from several odors like fear, worry, doubt, disbelief, gossip, and negativity. Do you have an odor?

In this passage, Paul is writing this letter to the church at Ephesus. During this time, there was a pagan temple dedicated to the Roman goddess, Diana. Sexual immorality and greed ran rampant during this time. As you continue to read this chapter, Paul is warning the believers in Ephesus to avoid these pitfalls. Paul instructs in verses 1-7 we must walk in love; in verses 8-14, he challenges us to walk in the light; and in verses 15-21, he challenges the people to walk in wisdom.

Paul states in verse 1, ". . . be imitators of God . . . ." The word "imitate" means to follow as a pattern, model, or an example. To "imitate" means to resemble, to reproduce, to produce a copy, or to mimic.

The church has an odor problem because we have patterned, modeled, resembled, copied, and mimic the world system. We have taken the odors of the world and brought them into the house of the Lord. We have no standards in our homes or schools, and it is becoming harder to differentiate between the church and the world systems. In the church, we are to practice and witness to our faith in Jesus Christ. In the world, our faith depends on man and woman's reactions. Instead of strategizing for the lost souls, feeding the homeless, and clothing the naked we encounter, we mimic the world and fall guilty by judging others by looking at their outward appearances.

I am a firm believer that we are to follow the example of God's action. One of my favorite childhood games was *Simon Says*. A designated leader would call out several commands and the rest of the group was responsible for carrying out the command. The leader would holler, "Simon says, 'stand on your right leg'" and we would stand on our right leg.

In this game, we would imitate the leader only if the command started with the words "Simon says." We need to imitate the Simon Says game and substitute "Simon says" with "God says." If God says it, then I believe it!

There is a theory in psychology called imprinting. Imprinting is a process occurring early in the life of a social animal in which a specific behavior is learned through association with a parent or a role model. In the world, we need more role models. As children of God, when we accepted Jesus as our personal Lord and Savior, we were imprinted with the mark of Jesus Christ. When we fail to imitate Christ, we neglect God's Word and what Christ has for us. As believers, we must grow in the faith that the word of God does not just rest on our lips, but is imitated in our life.

The passage continues to reveal that our odor problem is caused by neglecting to walk in love. As believers, we must be careful that we do not walk in the odor of control, manipulation, or selfishness, forgetting the gift of love.

I believe if you want to determine the odor of a church, examine the love of its members. "Love is the essential existence of every Christian. Love is the heart of the Christian faith, which is revealed throughout the Word. Love is the foundation of everything and anything worth-while."[43] Paul states we must "walk in love as Christ also has loved us and given himself up for us." Jesus' love for us is limitless. Christ proved that when He took all of our sins on the cross. It was Jesus' love that healed the woman with the issue of blood. It was Jesus' love that ate with sinners and the downtrodden. By His love we are saved, sanctified, and washed in the blood of the Lamb.

Eugene Peterson, the author of *The Message Bible*, explains love in simple terms found in 1 Corinthians 13:4-8:

> *Love never gives up. Love cares more for others than for self. Love doesn't want what it doesn't have. Love doesn't strut, doesn't have a swelled head, and doesn't force itself on others. Isn't always "Me first." Love doesn't fly off the handle, doesn't keep score of the sins of others.*
>
> *Love doesn't revel when others grovel. Love takes pleasure in the flowering of the truth. Love puts up with anything, trusts God always, always looks for the best, never looks back, but keeps going to the end. Love never dies.* [44]

Lori Beth James, author of *Jesus, CEO*, states, "If we all had x-ray vision – could we see the love by our human endeavors? Not what we say; but more importantly what

---

43 *Disciple's Study Bible,* New International Version, Holman Bible Publishers, Nashville, p.#1655.

44 Peterson, Eugene. *Message Bible,* NavPress, Colorado Springs, 2002, pp. 2085-2086.

we do. Our actions should speak louder than our words." [45]

Finally, we suffer from an odor problem because we have forgotten that it was Christ who offered and sacrificed His life as a sweet-smelling aroma. It was Christ who was hung high and stretched wide. It was Christ who was mocked, spit on, and ridiculed on Calvary's Hill. It was Christ who endured the suffering, shame, and pain. The scripture reveals in Romans 5:8, "God demonstrated his own love toward us, in that while we were still sinners Christ died for our sin." Paul writes in 2 Corinthians 2:15, "For we are to God the fragrance of Christ among those who are being saved and among those who are perishing."

Prayer

Lord, I pray that I do not have the world's odor. I pray that I am a sweet smell in your nostril. Amen.

45 James, Lori Beth. *Jesus, CEO*. Hyperion, New York. 1995, p. #256.

Reflection

Do you have an odor? If so, what odor is preventing you from being a sweet smell in God's nostril?

How do you show the love of Jesus Christ in your church and community?

My Action

Show the love of Jesus Christ by volunteering in a church ministry for a week during Lent.

March 21, 2020
Psalm 23

The 23rd Psalm is probably the most familiar psalm that I was taught as a child. This psalm has been universally attributed to the psalmist David and is a depiction of his own life. Interestingly, scholars have debated upon the actual time in which David constructed this passage of scripture. Theologians believe that he wrote this as an older adult. This premise is based on the range of experience covered in the psalm, the subdued tone, and the confidence that permeates throughout this text. Other scholars believe that this text was written when David was king and needed God's protection and deliverance. Another viewpoint argues that this psalm was written when David was sent in the wilderness at the time of his escape from Absalom.

However, when life has dealt me an ugly hand or when my way forward in life seemed unclear, I have found strength and hope in this passage of scripture. This psalm has been the model of God's provision and protection. This psalm has been the cornerstone of coping with and understanding the death of a loved one. This psalm has conquered fear, brought hope to the hopeless, and brought victory in the valley.

Several years ago, there was a controversial book on the market titled, *The Value in the Valley,* by author and life coach Iylana Vanzant. In her book, Vanzant challenges the everyday, hardworking woman to examine her valley experiences as a guide to conquer life's dilemma. She describes a valley as a life situation designed to teach a character trait or spiritual virtue that has been undeveloped or underdeveloped during the course of your life. She further states that valley experiences are purposeful. They open our eyes and strengthen our minds to teach us faith, strength, and patience. These are all essential mountain-climbing skills. Valleys come in many shapes, sizes, and disguises. There are many times we may fall into a valley without knowing how or understanding why.

According to Vanzant's definition of a valley, it could be a job you hate, a disruptive relationship, an addiction, an attitude, an obsession. A valley can be forgiveness, anger, depression, rejection, failure, criticism, confusion, or loneliness. A valley is usually dark and bleak. No matter how dark and bleak the valley seems, however, there is always a lesson to be learned from the valley.[46]

Several years ago, I chaperoned a confirmation retreat trip at Ben Hill UMC, in Atlanta, Georgia. We spent two-and-a-half days at Amicalola Falls, where we engaged the confirmands in various team building exercises and leadership development. During this trip, we were strategically placed in a valley and were left by the camp rangers to figure out how to return to the campsite.

As we all began at the base of the valley, the 23rd Psalm

---

46 Vanzant, Iylana. *The Value in the Valley.* Simon & Schuster Publishing. 1996.

popped into my head: ". . . even though I walk through the valley. . ." We began to walk. Our legs became tired and our bodies rapidly began to deteriorate. We all started by walking in the upright posture but along the path we began to show signs of heat exhaustion. As we walked, a few of the confirmands became ill and needed to stop walking. This problem was discouraging to some of the small groups because a prize was to be given to the group who completed the journey with the fastest time.

Several of us stopped along the way, only to realize that we were not getting any closer in completing our task or winning the prize. Some of the confirmands were sitting at the base of the valley complaining and murmuring because of the fear to move through this obstacle course.

There were several lessons we learned through this valley experience. First, we must keep moving. When you walk through a situation it means that you are not stationary; you are constantly in motion. You do not have the time or energy to feel sorry for yourself. The reality is that when some of us are faced with the valley experiences, we fold. We feel like we are caught between two mountains.

As human beings we think that valley experiences are always bad. I believe they are lessons for us to learn to depend on God for guidance and direction. The Lord doesn't always solve our problems in a hurry. God allows us to walk through the valley of the shadow of death. The phrase "shadow of death" translated in the Hebrew simply means "darkness." This translation does not necessarily mean death as in dying. But the valley of the *shadow of death* can refer to any distressing time in our lives – whether it is sickness, financial hardship, loss of job, disappointment, or any setbacks.

Secondly, I learned from the valley experience that the psalmist gives us hope by revealing that *God is with us*. The text states, "I will fear no evil; because you are with me." In the valley experiences, "God is our refuge and strength, a very present help in trouble" (Psalm 46:1). As believers we are adopted into the Kingdom. We cannot see through the darkness of the valley, so we are forced to trust in the Lord.

Finally, I learned from my valley experience that the psalmist encourages us that *God's rod and staff will bring comfort*. Ancient shepherds used the rod and staff. A rod was worn at the belt and the staff was used to walk and to round up the sheep. These unique tools were used to rescue, protect, and guide the sheep.

In the shepherd and sheep relationship, the sheep were never alone. The shepherd is standing over them guiding them to safety. The sheep depend on the shepherd to lead them to the water and to the pasture. The shepherd anoints the sheep's face with oil to protect the sheep from getting stuck in the thorn bush, as well as to prevent snakes from biting them in the grass. Sheep are social animals and they gather in flocks. Interestingly, the sheep will wander off, fall into a crevice, get caught in a thorn bush, or fall off a cliff. Sheep are curious and helpless creatures, and are unable to find their way home. David reminds us that "Thy rod and thy staff will comfort me." His words are our assurance as sheep that the Shepherd will never leave us.

Prayer

Lord, thank you for leading, guiding, and comforting me through my valley experiences. Amen.

Reflection

What image comes to your mind when you think of the shepherd and sheep relationship?

My Action

Take a long walk and recite the 23rd Psalm several times.

March 22, 2020

Fourth Sunday in Lent

My Personal Reflection Notes

Reflect on this past week.

What day stood out during this Lenten journey?

What did you learn about yourself and your relationship with Jesus Christ?

Which "My Action" of the week brought you great joy or struggle? Why?

Please journal your thoughts. (*Space is available on the next page for journaling.*)

March 23, 2020

Acts 9:1-20

How many times in our lives have we confessed to the Lord, "Lord, I feel like giving up?" or "God, give me another chance, I will get my life in order," or "Lord, if you help me with this problem, I promise I will start going to church again?" Have you ever uttered any of these statements or something similar? The Bible states in Lamentations 3:23 "that every morning we are granted new mercies because great is thy faithfulness." Isn't it sobering to know that every morning God's compassionate acts are faithful to God's people? We serve a God who will grant His children a second chance on life. If you are not convinced, let's examine the text for today where God granted a second chance to a persecutor of Christians to become a preacher of the gospel.

Saul, later known as Paul, would be classified as your modern-day gang banger. He was a Pharisee Jew, small in stature, knew the Bible, and trained under the best. He sincerely believed that the Christian movement was dangerous to Judaism. Therefore, he hated the Christian faith and persecuted any Christians in sight.

At the sound of the word "Christian" he would go absolutely crazy. He was a brutal man, and he approved and witnessed the stoning of Stephen and many others as recorded in Acts 8:3.

The scripture reveals that Saul gets permission to travel to Damascus to capture Christians and bring them back to Jerusalem. The text explains that a light from heaven came flashing around and Saul finds himself knocked to the ground. He heard a voice say to him, "Saul, Saul, why do you persecute me?" "Who are you, Lord?" Saul asked. Saul for the first time in his life was confronted with the truth of the gospel. He had a personal encounter with the Lord that enabled a second chance on life. "Encounter" as defined by *Webster*, means "to come upon face to face." Saul didn't have an encounter with just anyone. He had an encounter with the risen Savior "that borne our infirmities and carried our diseases, the risen Savior that was wounded for our transgressions and the risen Savior that is the chief cornerstone of our faith" (Isaiah 53:4). Scholars believe the literary importance and the theological complexity of Saul's Damascus road encounter with the risen Jesus is indicated by the fact that it is recounted three times in the scriptures. Here in the narrator's voice (Acts 9), and twice again in Paul's voice found in Acts chapters 22 and 26, Saul encountered the risen Savior.

Have you had a personal encounter with the Lord Jesus? Or when was the first time you remember encountering Jesus Christ? Was it at a worship service where the praise band was singing exuberantly, and the sermon preached was directed to you and your circumstances? Was it at Confirmation? Family and friends came from miles to witness you stand before the church, dressed in white to declare your faith. Or your Infant Baptism? Again, family and friends came from miles to witness the cold water sprinkled on your head as you smiled or cried. You really don't remember, but pictures were taken and your parents rehearsed the day in detail over and over.

I truly believe that an encounter with the Lord will result in a change of lifestyle. An encounter with the Lord will change your valley experiences into victories. Your hopeless situations will begin to be hopeful. We've witnessed this by the conversion of Saul to Paul on the Damascus road. Unfortunately, we live in a society where people cease to believe that "immediate" conversions still exist. The Bible states in 2 Corinthians 5:17, "Therefore, if anyone is in Christ, he is a new creation; the old things have gone, the new has come!" In the Bible, when individuals encountered the Lord, things didn't remain the same. When Adam and Eve encountered the Lord, God confronted them with their sin. When Abram encountered the Lord, God promised that He would be the Father of many nations. When Moses encountered the Lord, he had the burning bush experience. The encounter with the Lord was the vehicle that changed the rest of Saul's life, and enabled him to teach the gospel of Jesus Christ to the first-century world.

Prayer

Lord, I seek to see your face. I desire to have my personal encounter with you that will change my life. Amen.

Reflection

When people encounter you, what quality of Jesus do they walk away with?

Whose life are you changing?

My Action

During this Lenten season, volunteer at an elementary, middle, or high school in your community.

March 24, 2020
Psalm 146

One of my favorite courses in seminary was worship. I learned the importance of the elements of worship, but what I found most fascinating was the topic of praise. Praise is a powerful weapon in worship, which is underestimated. God is the origin and owner of praise. Praise moves us from our present reality of circumstances to God's presence. According to the *New Interpreter's Dictionary of the Bible*, "Praise is defined as the human activity, oriented toward others in a gesture of gratitude and exaltation for the person, accomplishments, and presence of others." The definition further enlightens me that "the unsolicited and unmerited character of praise brings joy, satisfaction, and builds bonds between those praised and the ones who offer praise."

When you examine the Bible, the most common Hebrew words for praise are *halal* and *t'hillah*. In both the Old and New Testament, praise is most often oriented toward God. Praise is a natural and necessary response to fully enjoy the object that is praised. Praise comes from a Latin word meaning "value or price." To give praise to God is to proclaim God's merit or worth. Praise is an act of worship. Our praise towards God is the vehicle by which we express our joy to the Lord. There are several ways to praise God. Praising God may be individual, collective, spontaneous, or arranged in a song or prayer formation.

I can testify that praising God helped me through my multiple hip surgeries last year. There were times in the late night or early morning that I would reach over and grab my phone and listen to my favorite artists on YouTube. The praise songs would allow me to focus on the Word of God and not focus on the excruciating pain or the spasms that would radiate down from my hip. Sometimes I found myself in tears and the only thing I could do was sing God's praises to bring me comfort and relief. Songs like "O Come to the Altar," "Tis So Sweet," "Made A Way," "Bow Down and Worship," "I Will Trust," "Reckless Love," and "Hills and Valleys" took on new meanings. I was confident that I was going to make it through this bizarre situation and there was no illness my Savior had not endured for me on the cross.

Today's passage of scripture, Psalm 146, is the first of the five psalms known as the Hallelujah psalms. This psalm focuses the reader to who God is and what God does. Praising God for who God is, is called *adoration*. Praising God for what God does, is known as *thanksgiving*.

The psalmist opens and closes with "Praise the Lord." The psalmist depicts God as our only real source of help and deliverance.[47] In verses 5-9, the psalmist depicts God as the faithful God who works for the oppressed, helps the needy, frees the prisoner, loves the righteous, heals the

---

47 Richards, p. #374.

infirm, watches over the alien, sustains the helpless, and frustrates the ways of the wicked.[48] Finally, the psalmist reminds us that the Lord is sovereign. God has no allegiance. God is always by our side, rooting for each of us.

Prayer

Lord, O how we praise you for being the Lord of the oppressed, who cares for the needy, the homeless, prisoners, and aliens. Lord in your mercy, hear my prayer. Amen.

Reflection

What does it mean that praise is an act of worship?

What does it mean that praising God is a constant attitude?

What praise song or hymn helps you through any tough situation?

---

48 Ibid.

My Action

Volunteer to serve in the worship ministry during this Lenten season.

March 25, 2020

Luke 1:26-38

When I read this text, I think of the song, "All Things Are Possible."

All things are possible
Cause I believe
Give me strength to find my way
As I journey through the day
Cleanse my heart, teach me to forgive
Fill my heart each day I live
Give me faith to just believe
You hear my prayer and know my needs
Lead me on till I find
A brighter world and peace of mind
All things are possible
Cause I believe in you.[49]

As we examine the text, the angel Gabriel brought a second birth announcement in the sixth month of cousin

---

49 Rotha, John. "All Things Are Possible [with lyrics] - Hillsong feat. Darlene Zschech." YouTube.com. https://www.youtube.com/watch?v=x_NcescDvdQ. Accessed August 16, 2019.

Elizabeth's pregnancy, this time to a young girl in Nazareth named Mary. The people in Judah did not like the Jews in Galilee and claimed they were "not acceptable" because of their contacts with the Gentiles there. According to the text, the angel told Mary: ". . . do not be afraid, Mary, for you have found favor with God. You will be with child and give birth to a son, and you are to give him the name Jesus."

The Greek word for "favor" means "benefits and special honor." When God has favor upon your life, you should expect the impossible. Society confuses God's favor with social influence. Society teaches us that influence is not *what* you know, but *who* you know. I have come to realize in life that I would rather have favor with God than influence with humanity. When God has favor upon your life, doors will open wide with opportunities.

The Bible records in Genesis 39:4 that God granted Joseph, son of Jacob, favor in Egypt and delivered him out of all his trouble. In Genesis 19:18, Lot found favor in God's eyes when God saved his life. Psalm 84:11 reveals, ". . . that the Lord will bestow favor and honor upon you. No good thing will God withhold from those who walk uprightly." To experience the possibilities, we must have a positive attitude of strong faith. God chose Mary for one of the most important acts of obedience. Haven't you found it interesting that on this Christian journey, our lives are based constantly upon our faithfulness?

As the mother of Jesus, Mary believed and obeyed. Believing the message from the angel, she considered it a blessing to carry the child conceived by the Holy Spirit. We could learn a valuable lesson from her faithfulness.

Mary was willing to be available to God. She could have resisted and complained, but instead she accepted her role. This young girl was faithful to the task. If you can see it with your natural eyes, then it's not faith. The Bible records in Hebrews 11:1, "Now faith is the substance of things hoped for and the evidence of things not seen." Faith is central to all of life.

Faith impacts how we live and walk with God. Faith enables us to please God. According to *Webster's Dictionary,* "impossible" means "hopeless, incapable of being done, unacceptable, unattainable, and unachievable." However, when my inabilities merge with God's divine capabilities, anything is possible!

Prayer

Lord, a virgin named Mary conceived our Savior, Jesus the Christ. That was impossible. May I grow so close with you that I follow by faith and not by my sight. Amen.

Reflection

How have you seen the Lord demonstrate favor in
your life?

Can you name an impossible moment in your life?
What happened?

My Action

Write down the things that you think God favored you
with today.

March 26, 2020
Ezekiel 1:1-3, 2:8-3:3

Are you willing to trust, obey, and go where God's will leads you? Do you feel that God has a special purpose for your life? Dr. Norman Habel, an Old Testament scholar, believes that a call is a summons by God to carry out a particular function. Habel believes that there are four stages in a divine call that are commonly displayed throughout the Biblical stories. He suggests that the call upon our lives has a direct correlation to these stages.

Habel believes: (a) there is a divine confrontation by God – a small voice, dream, or an unction of the Holy Spirit is leading you to do something, (b) there is the rejection of the call–where you wrestle with what God has revealed to you, (c) the assurance that God will be with you always, and (d) finally the acceptance of the call which leads to various responses.

I believe that everyone is called by God for a purpose. We are called as believers of the faith to go and make disciples of all nations, baptizing them in the name of the Father, and of the Son, and of the Holy Spirit. We are called as believers to a task of loving our neighbors as we love ourselves. We are called to help the downtrodden and needy by improving their quality of life. We are called to share our spiritual gifts with the body of Christ. We are called to stand up and fight the injustices of poverty, homelessness, racism, and sexism that we face daily. God is constantly at work bringing God's will to fruition. We are called to be ambassadors for Christ: to read, study, and apply the Word.

In today's reading Ezekiel, a priest, receives a vivid call from God in a vision. Then, we witness God calling the prophet to speak to the people of Judah for their rebellion and abstention to God's will. God instructs Ezekiel, "Speak my words to them, whether they listen or fail to listen." God admonishes Ezekiel, "Do not rebel like that rebellious house; open your mouth and eat what I give you." Ezekiel was commissioned to faithfully proclaim God's Word by eating the scroll. Can you imagine speaking to your own people who are stubborn and refuse to be obedient?

In 1994, I experienced my call to ministry at Ben Hill UMC in Atlanta, Georgia. I was sitting in the 11:45 a.m. worship service waiting for Minister Michael McQueen to proclaim the Word for the hour. I remember Minister McQueen stepping into the pulpit and reciting his title, "Are You Called?" Interestingly, Ephesians 4:11-13 was the epistle that accompanied his sermon. It reads, ". . . it was He who gave some to be apostles, some to be prophets, some to be evangelists, some to be pastors . . ." As he read the title and scripture, goose pimples rose up on my arms. At the end of the sermon Minister McQueen offered an altar call. The choir began to sing, and I don't know to this day how my body made it to the altar. As I recall, I knelt and heard the voice of God speak so clearly, "Go preach my Word." I couldn't fight back the tears or the desire to be obedient to God's will any longer. I felt a hand on my shoulder from the late Rev. Valerie Earvin. When I stood on my feet and turned to face the audience, half of the congregation was standing behind me with a look of approval. On February 13, 1994, I accepted my call to ministry, and the rest is history! As God calls, our responsibility is to respond and be committed to serve the Lord.

Prayer

Lord, thank you for the call on my life to be obedient, faithful, and committed. Amen.

Reflection

Do you feel that God has a call on your life to ministry? In what capacity?

Have you experienced the four stages of a call outlined by Dr. Norman Habel?

My Action

Take time to reflect and make an appointment to talk with a pastor, friend, etc., about next steps to fulfill your call.

March 27, 2020

Psalm 130

I was told a story about a pastor who was counseling a believer on a weekly basis. The believer would come into his pastor's office and bare his soul and his sins. The believer was ashamed of his sin, but unfortunately, he continued to commit this sin. At the end of their session, the pastor would have the believer pray. In his prayer, the believer would appeal to God for forgiveness over and over.

One day as they were ending their session, the pastor asked the believer to pray again. The believer started, "Lord, please forgive me, for this is the nineteenth time I've committed this sin." The pastor stopped him and said, "My son, this is the nineteenth time?" The believer replied, "Yes, sir." The pastor said, "Our Lord doesn't keep a record."

As you focus on today's text, the psalmist points out in Psalm 130:3-4, "If You, O Lord, kept a record of sins, Lord, who could stand? But with You, there is forgiveness." Isn't it wonderful to know that our God keeps no record of our sins? We confess, "God is faithful and just and will forgive our sins and purify us from all unrighteousness" (1 John 1:9). Through His forgiveness, our sins are erased and forgotten. When Christ died on the cross, He cleansed us from the weight of shame, guilt, and condemnation.

This psalm is classified as one of the Penitential Psalms (6, 32, 38, 51, 102, 130, and 143), stressing repentance and forgiveness of sins.[50] The first two verses (Psalm 130:1-2) reveal a passionate desire. The psalmist is crying out to the Lord to hear his voice and grant him mercy for his wrong doing. The psalmist does not explicitly confess sins, but such a confession of repentance is implied in verses 3-4.[51] "Repentance called for throughout the Bible is a summons to a personal, absolute, and ultimate unconditional surrender to God as Sovereign. Though it includes sorrow and regret, it is more than that. In repenting, one makes a complete change of direction (180-degree turn) to God." [52] The Bible reveals the importance of repentance: (a) God commands it, (b) it is necessary for salvation, and (c) it's the reason for the Messiah coming to the earth.

In Acts 17:30, Luke states, "God commands all people everywhere to repent." Luke 13:3 reveals, "But unless you repent, you too will all perish." No one is exempted from repenting. All must respond to God with repentance. The Apostle Paul writes in 2 Corinthians 7:10, "Godly sorrow brings repentance that leads to salvation and leaves no regret, but worldly sorrow brings death." Finally, Matthew 1:21 tells us the Messiah will come "to save his

---

50 *Disciple Bible Study Notes*, p. #737.

51 Gaventa, p. #345.

52 Wikipedia. https://en.wikipedia.org/wiki/Repentance. Accessed August 16, 2019.

people from their sins."

In Psalm 130:5-6, waiting with watchfulness is declared by the psalmist. The psalm ends in verses 7-8 with an appeal for the entire community to have hope in the Lord as the loving Redeemer.

Prayer

Lord, out of my distress I call out to you! I humbly ask for your forgiveness and repent of my sins. Amen.

Reflection

How have you experienced God as the loving Redeemer?

My Action

Read and reflect on all seven Penitential Psalms:

- Psalm 6
- Psalm 32
- Psalm 38
- Psalm 51
- Psalm 102
- Psalm 130
- Psalm 143

March 28, 2020

Luke 24:44-53

In my leisure time, I have always had a love for watching the *CSI* and *SVU* series as well as *Criminal Minds*. I don't know if it is my biology and chemistry background that takes over, or if it is the fascination in watching the scientists, medical examiners, and police strategically figure out a cold case. The turning point in every episode is when new evidence such as fingerprints, a DNA specimen, or a surveillance video is discovered. However, with all of the modern technology to break the case, there is something always critical about an eye witness.

An eyewitness is someone who has firsthand knowledge, not secondhand knowledge, and is testifying based on facts, not hearsay. I was once told that what an attorney looks for in a case is not only an eyewitness, but a "credible eyewitness." This reminds me of an anecdote I was told about "credible eyewitnesses."

About ten years ago during a homicide trial in New York City, the prosecution was examining a witness on the stand. In his testimony, the witness stated that he saw the victim lying on the ground, obviously dead.

When the prosecution had finished, the defense lawyer

rose to his feet with the intent on undermining the credibility of the witness and started cross examination.

The defense attorney began to ask a series of questions:

"Sir, are you a doctor?"

"No," replied the witness.

"Are you a paramedic?"

"No."

"Have you ever gone to medical school?"

"Never."

"Then tell me, sir, how do you know that the victim was indeed dead?"

"Well," responded the witness, "I attended his funeral two months ago."

In today's text, Jesus has been resurrected and appears to two people traveling to a village called Emmaus. After his encounter on the Emmaus road, Jesus then appears to another group of people, His disciples, making them eyewitnesses also. What makes these witnesses credible is written into Jewish Law: two witnesses authenticate truth. These eyewitnesses knew without a shadow of a doubt that the evidence proved that Jesus was the Risen Savior!

He told them, "This is what is written: The Christ will suffer and rise from the dead on the third day, and repentance and forgiveness of sins will be preached in his name to all nations, beginning at Jerusalem. You are witnesses of these things. I am going to send you what my Father has promised; but stay in the city until you have been clothed with power from on high" (Luke 24: 46).

Christ suffered; they witnessed the marks on his hands and feet. The resurrection verifies that Christ's death paid the full price for our sins. The scripture reminds us that "God demonstrated His love for us that while we were yet sinners Christ died for us." No one is exempt from sin. Paul reminds us in Romans 3:23, "All have sinned and fall short of the glory of God."

Christ made it possible for humanity to be reconciled into a right relationship with God by repentance. It is through God's grace, God's "unmerited favor," that believers are forgiven. Ephesians 1:7 reveals, "In him we have redemption through his blood, the forgiveness of sins, in accordance with the riches of God's grace."

This statement was affirmed in Acts 1:8b: "But you will receive power when the Holy Spirit comes on you; and you will be my witnesses in Jerusalem, and in all Judea and Samaria, and to the ends of the earth."

Jesus instructs His disciples that the mission is where they are, but their task is to be witnesses to the ends of the earth. The Holy Spirit was promised to His disciples through the indwelling Spirit of God. It is a power to feed the hungry, clothe the naked, and heal the sick.

After Jesus gave His Disciples the instructions, He was ascended into heaven. "Then they worshiped him and returned to Jerusalem with great joy" (Luke 24:52).

Prayer

Lord, allow my life to be a credible witness for Jesus Christ. Amen.

Reflection

Are you witnessing the Gospel of Jesus Christ to the "ends of the earth?"

My Action

Spend time in prayer with God on how God would have you to be a witness.

March 29, 2020

Fifth Sunday in Lent

My Personal Reflection Notes

Reflect on this past week.

What day stood out during this Lenten journey?

What did you learn about yourself and your relationship with Jesus Christ? Which "My Action" of the week brought you great joy or struggle? Why?

Please journal your thoughts. (*Space is available on the next page for journaling.*)

March 30, 2020

Acts 20:7-12

In 1994, there was a popular show called *Friends* that took place in New York City with a cast of three women and three men. Four of them all lived in the same apartment complex and faced the ups and downs of life and love in New York. The show lasted for ten years, and there was always something humorous about their friendships with each other or other people. Like any relationship, friendships take love, support, and work if you want them to survive.

Interestingly, Aristotle believed that there are three kinds of friendships: (a) *friendships of utility* exist between you and someone who is useful to you in some way, (b) *friendships of pleasure* exist between you and those whose company you enjoy, and (c) *friendships of the good*, which are those based on mutual respect and admiration.[53]

As we examine the Bible, we witness several examples of friendships and how we should treat each other. For example, consider Abram and Lot. Abram reminds us of loyalty and going above and beyond for a friend. Abram gathered hundreds of men to rescue Lot from captivity.

---

53 Kelly, Maura. "The 3 Kinds of Friendships." Marie Claire. https://www.marieclaire.com/sex-love/a4028/friendships-aristotle-utility-ethics-lifestyles/. Accessed August 12, 2019.

"When Abram heard that his relative had been taken captive, he called out the 318 trained men born in his household and went in pursuit as far as Dan" (Genesis 14:15). "Jesus had a close a friendship with Mary, Martha, and Lazarus to a point where they spoke plainly to him, and he resurrected Lazarus from the dead."[54] "'Lord,' Martha said to Jesus, 'if you had been here, my brother would not have died. But I know that even now God will give you whatever you ask.' Jesus said to her. 'Your brother will rise again'" (John 11:21-23).

According to Aristotle's views on friendships, one could deduce that the Apostle Paul's relationship with the Ephesian elders could fall into all three categories. Paul was useful to the new converts at Troas by teaching and exposing them to the Gospel. There was a mutual admiration and respect fostered between Paul and the Ephesian elders. The text reveals they definitely enjoyed each other's company as Paul engaged them in worship that lasted until midnight. Paul had been a resident of Troas for two years and was saying his final goodbyes. Remarkably, the story of Eutychus is often seen as comical, with a twist of tragedy, turned into a miracle. However, there are scholars who believe that Paul and the Ephesian elders model friendship and love. The respect and admiration of Paul's friendship is maintained because of his witness to the Jew and Gentile about the Gospel of Jesus Christ. Paul had been on a quest for two years sharing his Christian journey with the new converts. His life was transparent and his friendship was based on integrity. This is Paul's

54 Mahoney, Kelli. "Examples of Friendship in the Bible." LearningReligions.com. https://www.learnreligions.com/examples-of-friendship-in-the-bible-712377. Updated June 25, 2019.

last farewell speech to the Ephesian elders before he faces captivity. His speech covered warnings about the future, appointment of successors, encouragement to follow teaching, blessings, and prayer for those left behind.[55]

However, as the story unfolds, Eutychus falls asleep and tumbles from a three-story window to his death. Paul goes downstairs and throws himself on the body of Eutychus. Eutychus is revived immediately. Paul returns to his meeting place and continues to engage in worship until daylight. Proverbs 18:24 states, "Some friends play at friendship but a true friend sticks closer than one's nearest kin." Paul showed not only love and care for his brother Eutychus, but a deep witness to the people of Troas that one's life and spiritual soul were important.

Dale Carnegie, American writer and developer of famous courses on life skills, states, "You can make more friends in two months by becoming interested in other people than you can in two years by trying to get other people interested in you." Whether this text is a fascinating story or a model of friendship, the Bible reveals that "Greater love has no one than this: to lay down one's life for one's friends" (John 15:13).

Prayer

Lord, the world competes for all of my attention. Let my friendships be a model of love, care, and mutual respect and admiration. Amen.

---

55 Gaventa, p. #760.

Reflection

What do you value in your friendships?

There are several friendships in the Bible. Name a friend. Compare your friendship with a Bible friendship. What have you learned about the Bible friendship that can enhance your friendship?

My Action

Invite a friend that you have not been in contact with recently to breakfast, lunch, or dinner.

March 31, 2020

Ephesians 2:1-10

Amazing Grace! How sweet the sound
   That saved a wretch like me!
   I once was lost, but now am found;
   Was blind but now I see.

'Twas grace that taught my heart to fear
   And grace my fears relieved;
   How precious did that grace appear
   The hour I first believed.[56]

That is one of my favorite hymns/stories, and it helps illustrate today's passage. "John Newton, a sailor, faced a conversion experience when his ship, *The Greyhound,* had been in a tumultuous storm for over a week. On the eleventh day of the storm, sailor John Newton was tied to the helm of the ship and tried to hold the ship on course. Its canvas sails were ripped and the wood of one side of the ship had been torn away and splintered. With the storm raging fiercely, Newton had time to think. His

---

56 Newton, John. "Amazing Grace." Stanzas 1 and 2. 1779.

life seemed as ruined and wrecked as the battered ship he was trying to steer through the storm. John Newton had rejected his mother's teachings and had led other sailors into unbelief. However, March 21, 1748, was a day Newton remembered ever after, for 'on that day the Lord sent from on high and delivered me out of deep waters.' Only God's amazing grace could and would take a rude, profane slave-trading sailor and transform him into a child of God."[57]

Many of us are like John Newton as we are faced with the tumultuous storms in our lives. Our storms can take on many shapes and forms. The storm can be one of sin, family upheaval, losing a job or a loved one, and the list continues.

However, ". . . because of His great love for us, God, who is rich in mercy, made us alive with Christ even when we were dead in transgressions – it is by grace you have been saved" (Ephesians 2:4-5). The Apostle Paul reminds us in the text how our lives used to be and now how our lives can be. "Therefore, if anyone is in Christ, the new creation has come. The old has gone, the new is here" (I Corinthians 5:17).

Sin brings eternal damnation. When we live for our worldly desires and gratify the flesh, we are dead to Christ. However, God loved us so much that He didn't want us to wallow in our sins. It is by God's unmerited, unearned favor we have been saved. God sent His Son Jesus to give us the gift of life, which is salvation. Romans 6:23 states, "For the wages of sin is death, but the gift of

---

57 Christianity.com. "John Newton Discovered Amazing Grace." Used with permission. www.christianity. com/church/church-history/timeline/1701-1800/john-newton-discovered-amazing-grace-11630253.html. Accessed August 21, 2019.

God is eternal life in Christ Jesus our Lord." The Bible reveals in Romans 5:8-9, "But God demonstrates His own love for us in this: While we were still sinners, Christ died for us. Since we have now been justified by his blood, how much more shall we be saved from God's wrath . . . ." Being justified is the process by which sinful human beings are forgiven for their sins. Christ took our place on the cross. "God made him who had not sin to be sin for us, that in him we might become the righteousness of God" (2 Corinthians 5:21).

Our responsibility is to recognize that we have the power to conquer sin. Paul reminds us in Romans 6:14, "For sin shall not be your master, because you are not under law but under grace." Grace is based on faith and the law is based on works. Grace brings liberty and the law results in bondage. Believers are no longer under the law, but empowered by the Holy Spirit to live for Christ.

> *Through many dangers, toils, and snares,*
> *I have already come;*
> *Tis grace hath brought me Safe thus far*
> *And grace will lead me home.*[58]

Prayer

Lord, it is by your grace that I am saved. Amen.

---

58 Newton, stanza 3.

Reflection

How has God's amazing grace been exemplified in your life?

How has God demonstrated God's love for you this Lenten season?

My Action

Read aloud the hymn "Amazing Grace" by John Newton, written in 1779.

April 1, 2020
Psalm 143

Have you ever struggled with the question, *What is God's will for my life?* Even though the question seems straightforward, I constantly run across individuals who struggle with this topic. Oftentimes, individuals have a hard time discerning what the will of God is for their lives. People will go to great lengths to attend seminars, watch webinars, watch *Dr. Phil*, or read a multitude of self-help books seeking the answer to this question.

Today's reflection reminds us that when we experience tumultuous issues in life, the will of God should still be our primary goal. David begins this prayer by crying out to God for mercy and relief (verse 1). This intense plea for rescue is one of the places in the Bible where the connection is made between God's actions on behalf of the people and God's actions on behalf of the individual.[59] David realizes he has no right to expect God's help. Yet, his desperate situation filled him with dismay (verses 2-4).[60] As part of the prayer, the psalmist remembers God's miracles for the Israelites (verses 5-8). Even in distress

---

59 Gaventa, p. #349

60 Richards, p. #345

and uncertainty we must commit ourselves to be obedient to God's will. God's faithfulness is our hope in distressing times. In verses 8b-10, the psalmist is trusting God to show and teach him God's will. Finally, the psalmist is encouraged that God will bring him out of trouble in verses 11-12.

Through his own trouble, Paul has found directives that manifest the will of God in our lives, "Rejoice always, pray without ceasing, give thanks in all circumstances; for this is the will of God in Christ Jesus for you" (1 Thessalonians 5:16-18, ESV). The Apostle Paul has been giving words of encouragement and exhortation to the church in Thessalonica of how to prepare for the second coming of Christ.

Paul begins with "Rejoice always." Rejoicing is defined as the action of feeling joy or great delight. The joy required of the righteous person is produced by the Spirit of God. As believers, we know that joy is one of the fruits of the Spirit found in Galatians 5:22. There is a distinct difference between happiness and joy. Happiness depends on your daily mood or actions, but joy is an internal response. God never promises a trouble-free life, only that God will be there to comfort us through our troubles. The Apostle Paul writes in Philippians 4:4, "Rejoice in the Lord always, again I say rejoice." As Paul is writing from jail, he teaches us an important lesson: our inner attitudes do not have to reflect our outward circumstances.

Paul explains that in order to understand God's will for our lives, we must "pray without ceasing." I believe that effective prayer takes place when you have a loving relationship with the Lord. To pray without ceasing does not mean that every activity in life must be dismissed for the sake of prayer. But every activity must be carried out in an attitude of prayer which is the spontaneous outcome of God's presence. Prayer simply shows our total dependence on God.

Paul writes, "Give thanks in all circumstances for this is the will of God in Christ Jesus for you." Thanksgiving is an expression of our gratitude for what God has done and what God is doing in our lives. We should be thankful to God for all things, especially for the saving grace in our lives. It is easy to be thankful when things are going our way. Thankfulness is not a passive action but an active action. My mother would sing this song frequently as she worked: "Thank you Lord, Thank you Lord, Thank you Lord, I just want to thank you Lord."[61] As you go through your day, look out for the moments that make you feel thankful.

Prayer

Lord, my heart's desire is to be in Your Divine will. Amen.

Reflection

Do you feel you are operating in God's will?

---

61 Marshall, Judy. "Thank You Lord." 1975.

My Action

Find a hymn or song of praise that speaks to you to hum/ sing throughout the day.

April 2, 2020
I Samuel 16:11-13

Have you ever been overlooked? You felt you were the right candidate, but your coworker received the promotion. You wanted to be invited to the gala, but your invitation never came in the mail. You wanted to start in the football game, but the coach started the second string player.

In this week's passage of scripture, we witness David being initially overlooked by his father, Jesse, but then noticed by the prophet Samuel. As the story unfolds, God instructs Samuel to travel to Jesse of Bethlehem's house to choose and anoint the next King of Israel. Jesse introduces his sons to Samuel in birth order, beginning with the eldest, Eliab, and ending with the youngest. Samuel was impressed by Eliab's appearance and physique, but unfortunately, he was not God's choice. Jesse continues to introduce to Samuel his seven sons, but again, none of them were God's choice. Samuel then inquires, "Is there another son?" To Samuel's surprise, Jesse answered, "There is still the youngest, but he is tending the sheep" (1 Samuel 16:11). Jesse simply forgets David. He overlooks the youngest and smallest son.

Samuel patiently awaits the arrival of David, "who is ruddy with a fine appearance and handsome features" (verse 12). Then, the Lord compels Samuel to anoint David as the second King of Israel. Samuel anoints David in the "presence of his brothers and from that day forward the Spirit of the Lord came upon David with power" (verse 13).

No one likes the feeling of being left out. I can only imagine when David entered the house and saw the prophet Samuel, the reoccurring feeling of being over-looked was probably natural. What David didn't realize, was that his first meeting with Samuel would change his life forever. Even if we are feeling overlooked by humanity, we know that God has not overlooked us, and God has a plan for each of us.

David – a shepherd boy, a worship leader, and the slayer of Goliath – spent a lot time with God. God was preparing David in the field to be the second King of Israel. David was chosen because he had developed a relationship with God. According to the Bible, David was known to be "after God's own heart." God said about him, ". . . I have found David the son of Jesse, a man after mine own heart, which shall fulfill all my will" (Acts 13:22b). In Psalm 139:23-24, David prayed, "Search me, O God, and know my heart, try me, and know my thoughts: And see if there be any wicked way in me and lead me in the way everlasting." David's primary goal was to please God and be obedient to God's will. That's why we are shocked when God chooses certain people that do not fit the stereotypical image. God will surprise us and utilize the person who has been obedient to God's will. "But God chose the foolish things of the world to shame the wise; God chose the weak things of the world to shame the strong" (1 Corinthians 1:27). In this case, God chose the ruddy, youngest shepherd boy who didn't fit Israel's qualifications.

God values character over appearance. In 1 Samuel 16:7, the Lord said to Samuel, "Do not consider his appearance or his height, for I have rejected him." The Lord does not look at the things man looks at. Man looks at outward appearance, but the Lord looks at the heart. Every issue of life stems from the heart. Proverbs 4:23 reveals, "Above all else, guard your heart, for everything you do flows from it." In our western culture, we value outward appearance over character. People will spend money on expensive clothes, shoes, accessories, and makeup. People will spend countless hours in the gym trying to obtain the perfectly chiseled body. People will live extravagant lifestyles and travel on expensive trips only to impress humanity. However, God always looks from the inside out.

God values humility over haughtiness. James 4:10 reminds us, "Humble yourselves before the Lord, and he will lift you up." David was not a faultless man. He committed adultery with Bathsheba and murdered her husband Uriah. However, when David faced his sins, he repented, and asked God for forgiveness. He penned Psalm 51:4, "Against you, you only, have I sinned, and done what is evil in your sight, so that you are proved right when you speak and justified when you judge."

Prayer

Lord, when I feel overlooked let me remember that you are shaping, testing, and trusting me. Amen.

Reflection

Described the last time you were overlooked.

How did it make you feel? What did you do?

My Action

Read one of the psalms David wrote when he felt forgotten by God. Then write your own psalm to God.

April 3, 2020
Philippians 1:21-30

According to my calculations, there are 168 hours in a week. Many of these hours are spent commuting, working, eating, sleeping, talking on the phone, Facebooking, tweeting, tagging pictures on Instagram, and shopping.

With so many activities vying for our attention, how do we stay focused on the Gospel of Jesus Christ? In today's passage, the Apostle Paul gives us insights on how to live out our faith in the midst of the uncertainty in our lives. In a life dedicated to serving our Lord and Savior, Paul had faced false allegations, excruciating poverty, and illness. The Apostle Paul is locked in chains, writing from a Roman jail to a small group of believers residing in the Macedonian city of Philippi. The church had sent a gift with Epaphroditus for Paul. In response to their gesture, Paul wrote this letter to thank them for their gift, and to encourage them in how to live out their faith in the midst of trials and tribulations.

Paul reminds them to "conduct (themselves) in a manner worthy of the gospel of Christ, as well as to stand firm in one spirit and finally to strive side by side with one mind for the faith of the gospel" (Phil. 1:27).

What does it mean to "conduct yourself in a manner worthy of the gospel?" The Apostle Paul states in Ephesians 5:1, "Be imitators of God, therefore, as dearly loved children." To imitate is to follow as a pattern, model, or an example. God has chosen us to be Christ's representatives on earth and we are to live our lives consistent with the message of Jesus Christ.

I believe when you are an imitator of God you take on the nature of God. We are to practice and witness to our faith in God. Unfortunately, our attitudes and conduct in the church resemble boardroom negotiations. Instead of strategizing to bring all God's children into the fold of the church, fighting to beat the opioid addiction, and dealing with women's inequality, the church gets caught up in the nonessentials.

The Apostle Paul invites us to stand firm in one spirit. Theologian Dr. Cain Hope Felder states that, "The Apostle Paul is reinforcing an ideological position that encourages people to imagine themselves in a relationship of mutuality and relational indebtedness."

I believe when we examine mutuality and relational indebtedness in reference to women, there is nothing more powerful than women being of one mind: trusting, relying, and standing together unified in the precious name of Jesus Christ. The Apostle Paul sheds light on this in 1 Corinthians 12:12-13:

> *The body is a unit, though it is made up of many parts; and though all its parts are many, they form one body. So it is with Christ. For we were all baptized by one Spirit into one body whether Jews or Greeks, slave or free–and we were all given the one Spirit to drink.*

Despite our differences and our culturally diverse backgrounds, the unifying theme is our unrelenting faith in Jesus Christ. We don't lose our individual identities, but we have a fundamental oneness in our Lord and Savior. This oneness enables us to sing The United Methodist hymn written by Edward Mote:

> *My hope is built on nothing less that Jesus' blood and righteousness. I dare not trust the sweetest frame, but wholly lean on Jesus' name. On Christ the solid rock I stand; all other ground is sinking sand; all other ground is sinking sand.*[62]

Today's scripture states, "We are to strive side by side with one mind for the faith of the gospel." How much more can we accomplish for the kingdom when we strive side by side, being faithful to the gospel of Jesus Christ? It is so sad that we waste time and energy in the church and the world system of churches by fighting against one another instead of uniting. The Apostle Paul writes in Philippians:

> *Make my joy complete by being like-minded, having the same love, being one in spirit and purpose. Do nothing out of selfish ambition or vain conceit, but in humility consider others better than yourselves. Each of you should look not only to your own interests, but also to the interests of others. Your attitude should be the same as that of Christ Jesus.*
> **Philippians 2:2-5**

---

62 Mote, Edward. "My Hope is Built on Nothing Less." 1863.

Prayer

Lord, let me "conduct myself in a manner worthy of the gospel of Jesus Christ" daily. Amen.

Reflection

How do you conduct yourself in a world or church that faces a variety of divisions?

How do you strive for unity in the workplace, church, or community?

My Action

Seek out an intentional conversation about current issues of division.

April 4, 2020

Mark 10:32-34

I remember being called on January 10, 2014, by my brother-in-law. He told me to come to Kennestone Hospital, in Marietta, Georgia because my sister Wanda had taken a turn for the worse. As I entered the emergency room, a nurse directed me to her room. As I entered, Wanda was lying there in excruciating pain and my brother-in-law looked weary. As I stood holding her hand and trying to be encouraging, she uttered, "Y'all know I'm not afraid to die." Those seven words will never escape my mind. As sad as I felt, I was encouraged that Wanda was strong and courageous in her faith.

As you examine the text for today, Jesus is predicting His death to His disciples for the third time. Although there is no comparison of my sister's statement with the death of our Lord and Savior, I can only imagine how the disciples felt to hear Jesus predict His death again.

This time, however, the prediction was in more detail. He said, "And the Son of Man will be betrayed to the chief priests and teachers of the law. They will condemn him to death and will hand him over to the Gentiles, who will mock him and spit on him, flog him and will kill him.

Three days later he will rise." Nowhere do we witness in this text that the disciples understood or wanted to face Jesus' death. His words were meant to prepare His disciples for their journey without Him.

I believe Wanda's words were meant to bring us comfort and prepare us for the life without her. But how do we deal with these words: death, dying, and die? If we are honest with ourselves, these words make us feel uncomfortable. We feel awkward, nervous, sad, fearful, frightened, and sometimes even angry. However, as we grow in our faith, we know that death is imminent. Let us bring comfort to someone who is facing death, whether it is a listening ear, a shoulder to cry on, a loving hug, a gentle touch, or a calming spirit.

As believers, we must come to understand that death is the entrance into a new dimension of life with Jesus Christ. Christ has promised that He has prepared a place for you and me. The Bible reveals, ". . . do not let your hearts be troubled. Trust in God; trust also in me. In my Father's house are many rooms; if it were not so, I would have told you. I am going there to prepare a place for you. And if I go and prepare a place for you, I will come back and take you to be with me that you also may be where I am . . ." (John 14:1-3).

In this passage of scripture, Jesus captures the spirit of the place we call "heaven." He arose to prepare an eternal home for His followers to join Him. Isn't it comforting to know we have a permanent place with our Lord and Savior?

Is your life preparing you for the eternal reward? The

Good News is that the heavenly reward is not just for the people with great faith we read about in the Bible. The heavenly reward is for you who eagerly look forward to Christ's return.

Prayer

Lord, if I'm given the opportunity, allow me to bring comfort to someone who is facing death. Amen.

Reflection

Why does death make us feel uncomfortable?

Did the disciples understand the death and magnitude of Jesus' resurrection?

My Action

Volunteer in a hospital, nursing home, assisted living, or hospice for a day.

April 5, 2020

Sixth Sunday in Lent

My Personal Reflection Notes

Reflect on this past week.

What day stood out during this Lenten journey?

What did you learn about yourself and your relationship with Jesus Christ?

Which "My Action" of the week brought you great joy or struggle? Why?

Please journal your thoughts. *(Space is available on the next page for journaling.)*

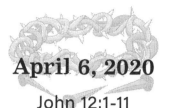

April 6, 2020
John 12:1-11

My father, Mr. Charlie Lewis Sr., born May 10, 1920, taught my siblings and me many life lessons. My father never missed an opportunity to impart wisdom into our lives. Some of his favorite topics were education, saving money, giving money, and sacrifices. He believed that everyone should obtain a degree and made sure that all of his children were college educated. He drilled in our heads that the principle of money is tithing 10 percent of your gross income, saving 10 percent of your gross income, and maintaining your lifestyle with the remaining 80 percent.

My father lived the scripture found in Acts 20:35, ". . . it is more blessed to give than to receive." I remember every Christmas my father would sit with my mother and think of gifts to give to the elderly or people who were less fortunate. After we would open our Christmas gifts and have dinner, he would load up his truck and deliver gifts to many folks in Statesboro, Georgia. He would always invite my brother and me to ride with him to deliver "a little Christmas blessing," as he would call it. I always wondered why. Why did Dad feel that it was his responsibility to give to the elderly or less fortunate? It didn't take too long realize that my father truly believed that it was "more blessed to give than to receive." To see the smiles and unexpected expressions on folks' faces not only gave my father joy, but the folks he blessed were extremely happy. The Christmas cheer ranged from money to food. This childhood memory of traveling around Statesboro on Christmas afternoon was etched permanently in my little spirit.

My parents collectively modeled a life of sacrifices. Words can't express how many times I saw the both of them sacrifice their time, energy, and money for the well-being of others. My parents' local businesses, Lewis Mart and Van Lines, were the gathering places for many to discuss the issues that faced the community of States-boro, Georgia. My parents would spend hours upon hours helping individuals deal with their problems. Many times, they gave money out of their pockets, fought for injustices, and helped young entrepreneurs start their own businesses.

My parents sacrificed for my siblings and me to receive a quality education. My mother earned an associate's degree. However, my father was not college educated. He was determined that his children would receive an under-graduate degree "to open more doors," as he would often express. He would always tell us that, "Your mother and I owe you a four-year degree; if you go beyond, you've got to pay for it." My father made many sacrifices such as bartend-ing for ten years at the country club in order to open up the first family business and educate his six children.

People sacrifice for those they love, and just as my parents sacrificed for their children, Mary sacrificed for Jesus in today's scripture. The *nard,* an expensive perfume used to anoint Jesus' feet, had a price tag the equivalent to a year's wages. Some scholars believe the perfume could have represented her life savings. The extravagance of Mary's action is an appropriate response to the costliness of what Jesus has done in bringing her brother back from the dead.[63] Mary's willingness to learn at Jesus' feet and the sincere faith she showed when Lazarus died was preparing her for Jesus' death. Her loving and selfless act of anointing his feet with perfume and wiping his feet with her hair "filled the house with fragrance."

Prayer

Lord, there is always something wonderful that comes out of sacrificial love. Let me show this love to humanity. Amen.

---

63 Gaventa, p. #723.

Reflection

What have you sacrificed in your life? What was the outcome of the sacrificial act?

Was there a great cost?

My Action

Think of someone who has sacrificed for you, and show your appreciation.

April 7, 2020

Psalm 71:1-24

Are you afraid of growing older? Many folks I know do not like the idea or thought of growing older. We expect aging to rob us of the joys of being youthful and full of life. There are special problems like aches and pains, bone breakage, and hearing loss that come with aging, making people less likely to look forward to it. The thought of these problems is like a dark cloud that hovers over individuals.

In the text for today, scholars believe that this psalm was written by David. It is thought that it is his prayer to God in his older years during the crisis of Absalom's rebellion. There are other scholars who believe that this psalm, because of a lack of title, was written by an older person in the community. The psalmist shares, even though he is older in years, his life has been built on his faith and filled with God's blessings and experiences. The Lord carries us from birth to death.

"For you have been my hope, O Sovereign Lord, my confidence since my youth. From birth I have relied on you; you brought me forth from my mother's womb. I will ever praise you" (verses 5-6).

"Since my youth, O God, you have taught me, and to

this day I declare your marvelous deeds. Even when I am old and gray, do not forsake me, O God, till I declare your power to the next generation, your mighty acts to all who are to come" (verses 17-18).

This psalm is classified as a lament and has the basic characteristics of one: (a) the psalmist always addresses God, (b) the psalmist states the complaint, (c) the psalmist expresses trust in God, (d) the psalmist asks God for help in this situation, and (e) the psalmist repeats confidence in God's help. This psalm falls into three parts, each ending on a note of soaring praise: verses 1-8, 9-16, and 17-24.

The psalmist's cries for help dominate the first four verses with phrases repeated in sequence: (a) deliver me, (b) rescue me, and (c) save me. This psalm is rich in images of God being our hope and refuge. God does not abandon or forsake the elderly. The psalmist realized that he had a lifetime of experiences that showed God's faithfulness in his life. God's faithfulness throughout past experiences causes us to trust and believe in God's Word. Proverbs 3:5-6 states, "Trust in the Lord with all your heart and lean not on your own understanding; in all your ways acknowledge Him, and He will make your paths straight."

As the psalmist continues to reflect in verses 9-16, the suffering and anxieties in life are remembered. The psalmist revealed that God had provided safety and protection in the midst of his enemies. He was under attack but realized that God would never leave or forsake him.

Finally, in verses 17-24, the psalmist reveals that even

in his old age he would still praise God for God's faithfulness and marvelous acts, God's faithfulness to deliver him from calamity, and even from the believer's death. This psalm is a teaching testimony of one wise with age, who has recorded these instructions for a future generation.[64]

Prayer

Lord, as I grow older, I thank you for sustaining, protecting, and delivering me from all evils. Amen.

Reflection

Are you afraid of growing older? What do you look forward to as you are aging? What do you dread in aging?

How has God been faithful in your life as you mature in your faith journey?

---

64 Gaventa, p. #329

My Action

Share this devotional with someone in a nursing home or assisted living. Ask them to share their testimony about their life.

Wednesday of Holy Week

April 8, 2020

Hebrews 12:1-3

*Therefore we also, since we are surrounded by so great a
cloud of witnesses, let us lay aside every weight, and the sin
which so easily ensnares us, and let us run with endurance
the race that is set before us, looking unto Jesus, the author
and finisher of our faith, who for the joy that was set before
Him endured the cross, despising the shame, and has sat
down at the right hand of the throne of God.*

Hewbrews 12:1-3 (NKJV)

During this season of Lent, how are you really
managing your daily life? Is Lent just a yearly habitual
act? Has it been difficult to pray, fast, reflect, or read
scriptures? Has this been a time of self-examination and
reflection? Have you learned any hidden nuggets about
Jesus Christ that parallels what you are experiencing? As
we examine our passage for today, how do we handle the
weights of the world and not become overloaded? How do
we handle sin? Do we master it, or do we take pleasure in
our sinful nature?

This letter to the Hebrews was probably written before
the destruction of the temple in Jerusalem in 70 AD.
Interestingly, scholars believe that this letter was written

to the Hebrew Christians, who were struggling with the new faith and considering returning to Judaism. They were chastised by the author because he accused them of remaining in their infantile spiritual state. The Hebrew Christians were struggling with Jesus. They were weighed down with old verses and new traditions. They were pressured with the decision to follow the old covenant of Judaism verses the new covenant of Christianity.

However, the author writes to bring comfort and to shed new revelation. He begins, "Therefore, since we are surrounded by such a great cloud of witnesses . . ." The author points to this great cloud of witnesses who are the named and unnamed faith heroes described in Hebrews chapter 11: these witnesses who have endured, these witnesses who have fought the good fight and finished the race, these witnesses who have borne testimony to the truth. As the author acknowledges the importance of our lifelines, he instructs us to "lay aside every weight."

A weight as characterized by Webster is "heavy, a load, a burden, pressure, or an overpowering force." A weight can be characterized as anything that holds you down, something or someone that dominates, manipulates, or controls your life. A weight can physically squeeze the life out of you, making it impossible to live and function as a whole person.

Take an inventory of this season. What weight or burden are you dealing with right now? What weight has you pacing the floor? Bishop TD Jakes writes that we must learn to lose these weights of the world, the relationships, and obligations that cling to you like secondhand smoke, poisoning the pure air you to need to survive and thrive.[65]

The text further enlightens us, ". . . and the sin that so easily entangles . . ." Can we talk about sin? We may be uncomfortable talking about it, but sin is a hard truth. It is as much a part of our lives as the air we breathe daily. We may try to ignore sin or pretend it's not there.

The text reveals, "We must run with perseverance the race that is set before us" (Hebrews 12:1). When I meditated on this text, the image of a runner always came to my mind. As the runner is running around the track, he or she knows the course that is set before them. However, the runner must stay focused and never give up or slack off. When we are faced with the weights or burdens of life, our first choice and inclination is to give up. Life will throw many curves at you along your journey. We may experience or have experienced carrying many loads or burdens. We may not know our exact course, but we do know as believers that the ultimate race that is set before us is Jesus Christ our Lord and Savior.

A runner may win a bronze, silver, or gold medal. As Christians, we are running with perseverance toward our heavenly reward. Paul states in Philippians 3:12, "Forgetting what lies behind and straining forward to what lies ahead, I press toward the goal for the prize of the heavenly call of God in Jesus Christ."

The author concludes in this text, "Fixing our eyes on Jesus, the pioneer and perfecter of faith. For the joy set before him he endured the cross . . ." During this Lenten season, I challenge you to keep your focus on Jesus

---

65 Jakes, TD. *Maximize the Moment,* G.P. Putnam's Sons, New York, 1999, pp. 49-50.

Christ. We look to Jesus as our connection that reconciled us back to God. Look to Jesus who lived and walked on this earth. In suffering and persecution, Jesus became our example. Paul writes in 1 Corinthians 15:12-14:

> *But if it is preached that Christ has been raised from the dead, how can some of you say that there is no resurrection of the dead? If there is no resurrection of the dead, then not even Christ has been raised. And if Christ has not been raised, our preaching is useless and so is your faith. More than that, we are then found to be false witnesses about God, for we have testified about God that he raised Christ from the dead. But he did not raise him if in fact the dead are not raised.*

Prayer

Lord, thank you for your son Jesus who died and endured the cross for my weights, burdens, and sins. Amen.

Reflection

What weights are you carrying that you need to unload?

What weights keep you from serving God?

How have you handled the suffering moments in your life?

My Action

Ask God to reveal your sin(s) that are preventing a closer relationship with the Lord. Then pray a prayer of repentance.

Maundy Thursday

April 9, 2020

John 13:1-17, 31b-35

I was once told a story of a man named James who worked as a superintendent of the City Rescue Mission for twenty years. He was asked in an interview, "Why have you spent your life working with dirty, smelly, drunken folks, who always promised to quit drinking but never had the will power or resources to stop?" He said, "All I'm doing is giving back to others a *little love* that God has shown to me."

As a young man, James had battled alcoholism for years. He couldn't pay his bills. He didn't spend any time with his children, let alone send them to college. As a result of his addiction, he lost his job, lost his friends, lost his children; he lost his self-respect, and finally he hit rock bottom by losing his family. In a drunken stupor, he wandered one day into a shelter for a bowl of chili. Interestingly, the church that was located down the street was responsible for not only the meal but the worship service for that evening. As the choir ministered, James didn't know if he was moved by the Holy Spirit or the Jack Daniels he had been drinking. He remembered the mood shifting as the preacher began to preach from Acts 9, the story of the Saul/Paul Damascus road experience. Then he heard the preacher say that God "was a God of second chances."

Before the sermon was over, James had drunkenly stumbled from the back of the room to accept the Lord Jesus as his Savior. Though his body reeked of alcohol and his clothes were filthy, he remembered feeling a weight lifted from his shoulders. James had a conversion experience that day in the shelter. Several years later, he began to seek God's will for his life. He felt the Lord calling him back to the place where he had been delivered, to reach the people still trapped by the spirit and disease of alcoholism. I believe that it was the power of God's redeeming love that enabled him to return to the rescue mission.

As we examine the Biblical passage for today, do we love as Jesus loved His disciples? How do we demonstrate love for our brothers and sisters? Do we recognize that love is a gift from God?

I would like to point out two factors for your reflection: 1) Love is the basis of Christian discipleship, and 2) Love is the motivation of Christian action. We recognize today as "Maundy Thursday." This is derived from Latin and means "a new commandment." Jesus said, "A new commandment I give you: Love one another. As I have loved you, so you must love one another. By this everyone will know that you are my disciples, if you love one another" (John 13:34-35). This scripture seems very simple. However, we live in a society that promotes what I like to call "the unholy trinity: me, myself, and I." There is nothing wrong with being self-confident.

However, we are ingrained since birth that "it's all about me." I believe that one of the greatest disappointments in society is that we have not been taught how to love like Jesus loved. If we loved like Jesus, the tragic events of mass shootings in schools, theaters, or public municipal buildings wouldn't happen. The "-isms of life" wouldn't separate the world. Poverty, homelessness, and domestic violence would be eradicated.

According to author Bill Long, love is both affective and effective. He characterizes love as a feeling and a way of treating others. It is the trait we should be identified by as Christians. We shouldn't be identified by the eloquent words we speak, how many scriptures we can quote, the crosses we wear, or the church we attend. We should be identified by the life-changing, unconditional love known as *agape*.

In John chapter 13, we witness Jesus washing the disciples' feet as an act of love and servanthood. He identifies His betrayer, and follows with the new commandment mandate. Jesus knew that one would betray Him, and one would deny Him. In verses 31 and 32, Jesus would be revealed as the Savior of the world by His death and resurrection. In verse 34, the loving of one another is reemphasized as the basis of the Jewish tradition found in Leviticus 19:18, to "love your neighbor as yourself." Loving one another is the basic recipe in living for Christ and advancing the kingdom. As we learn to love others, it proves our spiritual maturity and our relationship to God. We must come to recognize that the love of God has no boundaries, socioeconomic status, race, or sexual orientation. Love is a response. Love is a way of living that is made possible by God's grace through the working of the Holy Spirit. Jesus Christ reminded us in the text that the disciples were commanded to love one another with the same kind of love that they had experienced from Him. This would be one of the ways that they would be known as His disciples.

Additionally, love is the motivation of Christian action. The Apostle Paul reminds us in 1 Corinthians 13:

> *If we speak in the tongues of mortals and of angels, but do not have love, we are a noisy gong or a clanging cymbal. And if we have prophetic powers and understand all mysteries and all knowledge, and if we have faith, so as to remove mountains, but do not have love, we are nothing. If we give away all of our possessions to the poor and surrender our bodies to the flames, but have not love, we gain nothing.*

Paul is declaring we can have spiritual gifts and the faith to move mountains, but if we do not show love or have the motivation of love, then we are nothing. Everything we do must be motivated by the love of Jesus Christ: when we reach out to the least and lost, when we serve in our local churches, and when we sing God's praises. Love isn't a choice. It is a commandment that dates back to the Old Testament tradition.

Prayer

Lord, O how I love you. Let my actions be motivated by love. Amen.

Reflection

What motivates you to love your brothers and sisters in the faith?

How do you put your love into action?

My Action

Participate in a "Maundy Thursday" foot washing service in your community.

Good Friday
April 10, 2020
Psalm 22

Have you ever felt the silence of God? Have you ever questioned God's timing and wondered if God has forsaken you? Webster defines "forsaken" as "to renounce or turn away from entirely." Richard Foster, author of *Prayer: Finding the Heart's True Home,* states that "We will all experience in our faith journey a period of weariness and as a result our Lord and Savior [will] seem hidden or silent."[66] The question I would like for you to ponder today is, "What do you do when God appears to be silent in your life?"

Psalm 22 is a profound lament psalm that begins with a cry for help and concludes as a triumphant psalm of praise for God's deliverance. Interestingly, David speaks of his own distress and deliverance. Scholars have suggested that Psalm 22 is unique because verse 1a is quoted by Jesus from the cross, noted as the Fourth Word.[67] This psalm prophetically describes the crucifixion and resurrection of Jesus Christ. Scholars have suggested there are three main sections of this scripture.

---

66 Foster, p. #17.

67 See more about the Fourth Word here: https://biblehub.com/library/stalker/the_trial_and_death_of_jesus_christ/chapter_xvii_the_fourth_word.htm.

1. Verses 1-11 is an open cry, an exposition of the misery and mystery contained in the phrase "My God, my God."

2. Verses 12-21 develop the theme that trouble is close, with the disturbing description of the trouble in the lives of David and Jesus Christ.

3. Verses 22-31 move from a prayer for help to a song of praise that connects the fate of the psalmist David with the Messiah. In short, Jesus lives like the psalmist, as one of the afflicted. God loves the afflicted and God shares in our suffering.

David introduces this psalm by expressing these words, "My God, my God, why have you forsaken me? Why are you so far from saving me, so far from my cries of anguish? My God, I cry out by day, but you do not answer . . ." As I examined this passage closely, I recognized David's painful sense of separation from God at a time of trouble, similarly to when we feel that the Lord is silent in our lives.

When you feel that God is silent, you must pray through the period of silence. Prayer is the discipline that guides us into a constant communion with God. Prayer has power over everything. The Bible declares that ". . . the prayer of a righteous person is powerful and effective" (James 5:16). To understand prayer, one must pray. Prayer is hard work, but our communication with God is essential to our spiritual welfare. "Prayer involves ordinary people bringing ordinary concerns to a loving and compassionate Father."[68] Thomas Steagald, author of *Praying for Dear*

---

68 Foster, p.#10.

Life, states that "Prayer is a reason to rise in the morning; the strength for the day and the courage to face the night."[69] Prayer creates, redeems, and sustains us. Prayer is my life line to God. Prayer gets us to a place of peace in understanding: I can't, but God can.

Oswald Chambers, author of *Utmost for His Highest,* states as "Christians we must learn to trust God through our convictions and experiences, until we come to the point in our faith where there is nothing between God and ourselves."[70] What I found interesting in the text of verse 3 is that David says that "my fathers trusted in you." David confesses his faith in the God of his Fathers. God had been faithful to earlier generations. Surely, God will continue to be faithful to those who called upon His name. The word of God assures us to "trust in the Lord and lean not to your own understanding, always acknowledge Him and He will direct your path" (Proverbs 3: 5-6).

Even when you feel that God is silent, you can still trust God with the outcome. Trust is confidence in the character of God. Webster describes "character" as the "nature, quality, temperament, disposition, moral fiber, and spirit of a person." When you know God's character, no matter what confronts you, you have the ability to walk by faith and not by sight. God is consistent with His nature. God's character never varies. "Every good and perfect gift is from above and comes down from the Father of the heavenly lights" (James 1: 17). God's character cannot be contrary to his nature.

69 Steagald, Thomas. *Praying for Dear Life.* NavPress, Colorado Springs, 2006, p. #13.

70 Chambers, Oswald. *Utmost for His Highest.* Discovery House, 2017.

When you feel that God is silent, you must stand on the promises of God. The Bible declares that "God will never leave or forsake us." We must stop expecting people to solve our problems and STAND on God's words. Alexander Hamilton stated, "If you don't stand for something, you will fall for anything." So why not stand on God's Word that is faithful and true?

Prayer

Lord, there have been moments in my life that your silence has alarmed me. I know when I experience these times, I must pray, trust, and stand on your Word. Amen.

Reflection

Have you ever felt that God was silent? When?

What scripture(s) helped you through this moment?

My Action

Attend a Good Friday Service in your community.

Holy Saturday
April 11, 2020
John 19:38-42

When you were growing up, did you have any childhood fears? Fear of what might be under the bed, of weather changes, of peers not liking you, or some other fear? One of my fears that I eventually overcame was the fear of a monster in the closet. It took me months to realize that the reflections were only clothes hanging in my closet. Sometimes I would experience my body freezing up and my heart rate or breath quickening, and occasionally I would let out a fearful emotional response like a scream.

The monsters in my closet were fake, but for the early Christians the threat of persecution at the hands of the Jews was real. In today's reflection, we witness how Joseph of Arimathea and Nicodemus overcame their fears of the Jews during the process of Jesus' burial.

As the text opens, Joseph of Arimathea cast his fear aside and "asked Pilate for the body of Jesus" (John 19:38). As required by Jewish law, Jesus' burial was on the same day as His crucifixion. In asking for Jesus' body, Joseph of Arimathea, the secret disciple, was finally proclaiming that Jesus was the Messiah. "With Pilate's permission he came and took the body away." Joseph of Arimathea was accompanied by Nicodemus, "who earlier had visited Jesus at night." Nicodemus, the nighttime disciple, finally was ready to demonstrate his loyalty to Jesus.

John tells us that Nicodemus was the preparer of the myrrh and aloe mixture that weighed seventy-five pounds. "So they took the body of Jesus and bound it in linen cloths with the spices" and later buried him in the new tomb. Scholars believed they buried Jesus in the new tomb: (a) because the tomb was owned by Joseph of Arimathea, (b) because to be buried in a tomb not yet used was a special honor, reserved only for the wealthy and the kings of Judah, which perhaps was a reference to His royalty, and (c) some think the new tomb was emphasized by John so that after the resurrection there could be no mistake in the identity of the burial place.[71]

What happened to these men? Why did they decide to change their position? Could it be they realized that this "body" was actually "Jesus?" Jesus, who "healed the sick, raised the dead, cured those with leprosy and casted out demons . . ." (Matthew 10:8, New Living Translation).

As we see from the scripture reading, fear has always been a challenge we as humans have had to grapple with. What fear currently has you crippled? Depression, unexpected tragedy, deportation? In this unsettling society, how do we conquer our fears? How do we see our brothers and sisters as human beings in the Kingdom of God? How do we maintain our sanity in the midst of our fears?

---

71 Trusting in Jesus. *The Burial of Jesus.* https://www.trusting-in-jesus.com/burialofjesus.html. Accessed August 16, 2019.

Prayer

Lord, your Word reminds us, "for God has not given us a spirit of fear, but of power and of love and of a sound mind" (2 Timothy 1:7, NKJV). Amen.

Reflection

What was your childhood fear? How did you overcome it?

In this unsettling society, how do you conquer your fears?

My Action

Identify your fear(s) and begin to work through a process of eliminating your fears. If therapeutic counseling is an option, please inquire.

Resurrection of the Lord
April 12, 2020

Reflect on this past week.

What day stood out during this Lenten journey?

What did you learn about yourself and your relationship with Jesus Christ?

Which "My Action" of the week brought you great joy or struggle? Why?

Please journal your thoughts. After this Forty-Day Lenten Study, what has been greatest the lesson learned?